Winning the
Staffing Sales Game

Winning the Staffing Sales Game

The Definitive Game Plan for Sales Success in the Staffing Industry

Tom Erb

Library of Congress Control Number:		2017916673
ISBN:	Hardcover	978-1-5434-6148-0
	Softcover	978-1-5434-6146-6
	eBook	978-1-5434-6147-3

Printed in the United States of America

Rev. date: 11/21/2017

To order additional copies of this book, contact:
Xlibris
1-888-795-4274
www.Xlibris.com
Orders@Xlibris.com
763848

CONTENTS

Foreword

by
Jason Leverant

I was honored when asked to write a few words about Tom Erb, the author of this book and a well-respected leader in today's dynamic and fast-growing staffing industry.

First, I'd like to note that Tom is personable and easy to reach. He goes with the flow, which makes him really easy to work with. This quality, alone, makes him a standout as a trainer and leader in the staffing industry. As I've watched him work, I've seen how well he adapts to any situation, whether in a networking event or working with potential prospects. He's always on-his-game.

Tom really stood out when we were looking at different trainers. As a franchisor with one of the nation's leading franchise-based staffing companies, I wanted someone to come in and basically re-work our entire training system. As a company, we were looking for someone with a training concept that would create replicate-able processes, processes that could take someone coming in cold – somebody without any staffing experience – and run them through a process that would, quickly and effectively, produce a staffing-sales or recruiting professional.

It was a tough act. Everyone is striving for that kind of training. I say this because if you can pull talent from different industry types - including college graduates and people from other professions - and turn them into staffing professionals with your training, you can more quickly and effectively grow your business.

While we were looking at everyone out there for guidance, the one name that kept coming up was Tallann Resources, Tom Erb's company. I recall how one of our largest franchisees came up to me during a networking conference and said, "You've got to talk to Tom Erb. He's what you're looking for." I asked why and understood when I heard the answer: Tom has a background in staffing franchising, he's super successful, he has been a successful trainer for years, he has positioned himself as a leader in the staffing industry, and he had created a renowned series of process-driven programs for sales and recruitment. Tom and his programs were exactly what we were looking for.

For us, it was a perfect fit from the start. His processes address the complex, consultative sale of a service, which is vital in my business because staffing really is an intangible. We're selling the service of matching a job-seeker to a job, which incorporates a kind of middle-ground, a gray area. In other words, staffing isn't a hard, tangible product, so it takes skill and training to be successful, and the more quickly those intangibles can be learned, the faster a trainee can become effective.

As you are about to discover in the upcoming chapters of this book, with Tom's process you will be able to simply open the book, walk through the processes, and jump-start – or re-energize - your career as a successful staffing professional.

While we needed the kind of fast, replicate-able process Tom put together for our industry, I think you will soon appreciate the (tangible) fact that you can now hold that process in your hands - as you study the transformative methods in this book. I've watched trainees follow Tom's process and when they break through the program - through e-learning, circular trainings, or his sales-touch campaigns – they see how his easy-to-follow processes can make a difference in their careers. Companies see it directly through new client relationships, new pricing agreements and contracts, and ultimately, increased revenues.

For us, the learn-ability and replicability of his process is a great fit for us as a franchisor – we need that "model" for our owners and staff to follow. After all, replicability is what franchising is really all about, like coming up with a successful recipe for a major restaurant chain – which is hard to apply to staffing because we don't have the kind of product people can sink their teeth into and enjoy.

Well, Tom finally gave us something tangible and you can hold it in your hands. You can scroll through its pages. As you do, upcoming chapters will also reveal the fundamentals of a kind of universal process, one you can plug into virtually any market, for the benefit of virtually any salesperson in any industry.

Absorb the principles in this book and know that Tom Erb is the hands-down, go-to guy when it comes to all levels of training in the staffing industry. The really influential people in our industry will mention three, maybe four, trainers in the nation. When they do, Tom's name comes up as one of the most highly regarded for one primary reason: he has direct industry experience, he's not reciting theory. His processes apply a real boots-on-the-ground kind of practicality because he has actually done virtually everything he talks about in his programs, and with exceptional success.

If you're looking for a take-away, here it is: *The invaluable formulas in this book are not coming from somebody simply preaching another theory.* They come from somebody who:

-cold-called across a huge customer base
-negotiated contracts with prospective customers
-did the submissions
-learned by doing

…Not like somebody who read a couple of books and came up with a theory showing how he can do it better.

As you study the proven success formulas in this book, it's important to remember that Tom shares the experience of being in the moment, on the job, facing the challenges staffing professionals tackle every day. That's the difference and that's what stands out to me, along with Tom's humble, down-to-earth integrity, and his genuine interest in helping people learn to succeed. He's never cocky and always approachable, which changes the dynamic if you've ever dealt with a consultant with a superstar mentality.

Tom is always 'right there' for the trainee. He has lived the issues and has the answers. He makes the learning process an enjoyable, hands-on experience with real-world applications, and his methods work…time and again. It has been proven!

That said, thank you for allowing me to share my insights about one of the best in our industry. His integrity will show in upcoming pages and I hope you enjoy them as you learn to profit in the staffing industry. Happy staffing!

Yours Very Truly,

Jason Leverant

About Jason Leverant

Jason Leverant is President and CEO of the nationally renowned "AtWork Group" - more formally known as AtWork Franchise Inc. and based in Knoxville, Tennessee. With over 90 branch locations in 26-plus states and $300-plus million in annual sales, Jason's AtWork Group is a franchisor of staffing services, which excels in assisting people interested in becoming part of the fast-growing, dynamic staffing industry. For the past four consecutive years, Jason has been a member of Staffing Industry Analysts' prestigious "Staffing 100" list, which is comprised of the 100 most influential people in the staffing industry, and he was recently named "Volunteer of the Year" by the American Staffing Association.

Introduction

The art of the sale often seems to come from an elusive recipe, with wins and losses sometimes determined by what would appear to be sheer luck – good or bad – and success relegated to a numbers game tied to a random, 'shotgun' approach.

After years in the trenches of sales and marketing, from sales training to consulting for hundreds of the top companies and corporations in the staffing industry, I visualized a process that would absolutely work for almost anyone. The process would be <u>anything-but</u> random and it would create more consistency with explosive growth in closings… many times over mere shotgun selling (which, in itself, can exact a toll on production).

For many years I'd been watching too many highly motivated, talented sales professionals spiral downward into that dreaded periodic drought, sometimes leading to outright burnout - and all because they were stuck in a shotgun kind of numbers game. In this era of complex, multiple variations of communications and messaging systems, I knew we needed something more dependable than just random enthusiasm and relentless energy.

To succeed long-term and build a rewarding, prosperous career, we needed a reliable system of manageable outcomes to create a consistent flow of results for both sales people and their companies. After all my years of consultative sales and sales training - for some of the most powerful staffing organizations in America - I was able to develop just such a process.

Read this book from beginning to end, utilize every tactical tip and method within, and you will own that process.

Structure on Steroids

My system incorporates a structured, dependable schedule of activities and techniques, and a tactical re-design of the way we re-think our approach to opportunities. My structured process is designed to keep your momentum, and <u>every single one</u> of your opportunities, on track. This will enable you to maximize the potential of everything in your pipeline. And when this happens, consistency creates steady, dependable results, while your **income**…well, let's just call my process "**structure on steroids**."

With that, you need the kind of power-pipeline that will manage an incoming flood of new opportunities. We'll be talking about <u>my</u> kind of pipeline in this book, and why it effectively provides the right level of infrastructure for building long-term-manageable results – week to month, year-in, year-out.

Back to some of the gifted sales people who fell by the curbside: it wasn't their ability or sense of commitment that fell behind. The real culprit was their "methodology" and a slowly debilitating kind of internal attitude. Whether they would admit it or not, the people I'm talking about (in many cases fed by their managers) had subconsciously developed an unrealistic expectation of immediate results. In other words, they would place a call to a prospect, deliver a pitch, and actually expect the prospect to immediately make an appointment. Or worse yet, they left a message and wondered why the prospect didn't call them back. If they failed to get results the first or second time around, they would toss out the opportunity, chalk it up as a loss and move on. But after a few rounds in the toss-and-loss cycle, they started to become impatient and demoralized. Then it was time to dive back into a not-inexhaustible list of new prospects. And if those ones failed to produce an immediate sale or appointment, these dogged warriors would again move on, each time a little more dejected.

Sometimes the scattergun approach would work. Sometimes probabilities (or more often blind luck) were in their favor and the old "numbers game" would give somebody a good month or two of commissions. But more often than not and with this kind of methodology at work, I watched too many promising people wind up with too little - too late - to meet their goals, stay employed, and ultimately build the lifestyle they wanted. At some point, I'd seen enough and began to develop the process you are about to discover in this book

Honed and Proven

Since then, we have painstakingly developed a proven sales structure, which is implemented within a matrix of activities and goals that produce astounding, consistent results! For the very first time, I now present the building blocks upon which you can create a selling powerhouse of your own. Once in place, I think you will discover the full potential of the simple, strategic methodologies in this book. When you do, your production will have unlimited potential.

Before Consultative Selling

So what about traditional methods? You will still put them into play when the time is right. I'm just going to change the timing.

So many sales books and sales training programs focus on what to do… once you have the appointment. They focus on overcoming objections, negotiating and managing the sales process, and closing - all of which you certainly need to know. For example, many of the most popular, successful sales programs are all about "consultative solutions selling," which is a critical sales concept, but, once again, it's not much help until you find a way to get your foot in the door.

But first, how do we progress to the golden moment when we have our "foot in the (proverbial) door?"

Aha! That's what much of this book is really all about: how to turn essentially nothing — meaning an empty flow chart - into a healthy pipeline of "suspects," some of whom turn into "prospects" and, later, into solid "targets." Once your prospects become what I call "targets," then its time to let your traditional sales experience kick in and utilize all the solutions selling techniques you've learned.

That's another key to success: untold future opportunities. We'll get to that.

Let the Process Do the 'Heavy Lifting'

Like utilizing a winch for lifting an otherwise impossibly heavy load, my structured sales process will do most of the heavy lifting for you. Once you initiate, the results can be nothing short of astounding because this simple, manageable process allows your sales playing field to go virtually <u>viral</u> overnight.

That's the pitch. Now, let's put it into practice and make it WORK.

CHAPTER ONE

The Importance of a Structured Sales Process

Having a structured sales process in place isn't just important - it can quickly grow your income exponentially, achieve maximum results for every opportunity, ensure tracking and development of those opportunities <u>and</u> build consistent, gap-free production – for you and your company. Structured selling is a <u>must</u> in today's communication-saturated world, and the evidence for that begins with the decline of the old-fashioned cold call.

Death of the 'Cold Call'

Most sales veterans will tell you that selling has become increasingly difficult when cold-calling by phone. Some say it could become nearly impossible in a few years, and, if current trends continue, statistics support that claim.

From the 1950s through the 1990s and into the early 2000s, phone rooms and cold-calls ruled the day…until a communications revolution changed the rules. Yet, amazingly, most sales departments STILL rely on cold-calling, and when it won't work, their sales people are told to hunker down and call some more! After reading this book, you'll understand why *their* misfortune will work to *your* advantage. But before I show you why old selling methods have become less and less effective, let's look at some stats:

Recent studies show a current cold-call ratio of as much as 22 to 1, meaning that we average 1 live connect for every 23 attempts – the other 22 go into voicemail. Going back to 2000 when I first started in sales, my live connect-to-voice mail ratio was 6 to 1 – and even that felt like I was spinning my wheels!

So, let's think about this. Over the same period of time - from 2000 to present - we have essentially become 73% less productive doing the same, exact sales activity! And that means only one thing: Through no fault of our own as sales people, we can no longer expect to sustain a successful career if we ignore the facts and remain stuck in the cold-call rut. Voice mail-to-real person connections have deteriorated from an average 6-to1, back in the day, all the way down to 22-to-1 at this writing, and the plummeting spiral continues for the traditional cold call.

Cold-Call-Killing Technology

A number of factors have led to the "cold call corrosion" phenomenon, but the major culprit is Caller ID. Back in the day, Caller ID was something of a novelty. Now, everyone has Caller ID, and our prospects regularly use it to screen their calls. They hear the ring tone, glance down at Caller ID, and - right then - they make a snap decision about whether or not they want to pick up the phone.

Other cold-call corrosive factors abound. As indicated earlier, people are slammed by swarms of new communications. Today, we can't leave our smart phones alone. We utilize them to get regular phone calls and voice mail, emails and text, social media, instant messaging, spam advertising, junk mail - and all these different mediums leave people vulnerable to the non-stop bombardment of an endless river of communications… wanted or not. No wonder people look with increasing wariness at Caller ID when you make that call. Look at it from their perspective: These people are actually *protecting their time* from yet another robo-call containing somebody's sales pitch, political message…you name it: somebody wants to avoid it.

So, how can you make your call appear to be worthy of their time? *We're going to talk about that shortly* because your approach to selling is about to take a refreshing new turn. As you apply the principals in this book, the few calls you make will take on increasing importance as your contact level progresses through the structured sales process. As it does, you will begin to see a powerful new transformation as you elevate your contact from "suspect" to "prospect" to "target"…to a win.

But first we need to accept that fact that **people are generally moving away from the use of desk phones and even voice mail altogether**.

Coke Abolished Voice Mail

Yes, it's true, believe it or not. In 2014, Coca-Cola surveyed their corporate employees and posed the following question: "We're thinking of getting rid of voice mail. Would you like to keep it or get rid of it altogether?"

Get ready for a shock. After survey results were complete, it came out that <u>94% of corporate Coca-Cola employees said, "Get rid of voice mail."</u> Call into Coca-Cola's corporate office today and you can't leave a voice mail! And Coke isn't alone in the escalating, anti-voice mail/phone crusade. Over half of JP Morgan Chase's non-client interacting employees have voluntary opted out of having voicemail. Google has several corporate locations where they don't even have desktop phones. Now, you take your favorite device to work for your all your communications, including cell phones, notepads, laptops and the rest.

One problem with leaving the traditional voice mail is insecurity. After leaving a voice mail, have you ever asked yourself: "Have I said the right thing, in the right way? Should I review the message and re-record?" If you're like a lot of people, you might feel tasked to re-record a simple voice mail *five times* or more to get it right. What a waste of time! Most people are looking at email, text and social media as a more efficient means of communication, but even emails aren't safe anymore. I'll explain why in upcoming chapters of this book.

Millennials (and non-Millennials) <u>Ignore</u> Voice Mail

I was at a conference that talked about how millennials differ from other generations. Represented on the panel was a millennial who bluntly stated that <u>she doesn't even check her voicemail!</u> She then admitted that she'd been watching her voicemail light flash since she started working for the company. *Then,* she said that her voice mail box has been full since her job began, because she never listened to a single one.

And all this while she was sitting beside the president of her company, talking openly about what to some people sounded like gross negligence of her job duties!

But we need to understand that we now have a whole generation of working individuals who don't like, or value, voice mail as a communication method. They basically ignore it. Obviously, people are moving away from voice mail. They ignore incoming calls seen on Caller ID. AND we're seeing this more and more across generations, who tell me, "Yeah, I'm the same way." They won't even make excuses anymore. Now, they just say it, flat out: "I don't check my voice mail."

As sales people, we need to understand that this is the reality of communication now and moving forward. Regardless of the generations we are calling on, our prospects have to find ways to work more efficiently and filter out communication. For people in sales the message is simple: see it, get over it, use it to our advantage and adapt. Understanding this new reality allows us to re-adjust our pipeline communications accordingly. I will show you how in a moment.

Buyers' Habits are Changing Fast

As sales people, we need to do the same thing. For decades, the Number One way sales people had been trained to sell was simple - pick up the phone and make phone calls – but this is becoming less and less and less effective and the trend is going to continue. At the same time, people and their <u>buying habits are changing across the board, among all generations</u>. If we think about it, because the internet is so prevalent - because it has become such a big part of how people make decisions - how can we expect to get an appointment, or an instant job order over the phone, by simply picking up the phone and making a call? This has become an unrealistic expectation, because people just don't buy that way anymore.

Today when most of us look at making a major purchase, we get on the internet and do some research. We research the product or service, read customer review, and even poll our friends on social media. This alone marks a major shift in the way we do business as consumers, and most of this change has occurred over just the last few years. Given the ability to research virtually anything under the sun, people no longer make immediate decisions about what they buy. So, in sales, we must take that into account as well, knowing that <u>most people feel that they have to do some research before they buy</u>.

The Art of Variable Repetition

As an outgrowth of that trend, we now know that we need to have consistent, yet variable communication to lead to a sale. You need to master the "Art of Variable Repetition" to build a sense of comfort and familiarity with your contact. As you do, you will understand why it has become less and less effective to sell when simply picking up the phone to deliver a pitch. More importantly, it's only going to get worse. So now is the time to change.

I'll go into the finer points of Variable Repetition in later chapters, but for now, just know that a more refined method of making repeated contact is the way to go. Here's why…

Where Your Cold Call Ranks on
a Prospect's Priority List

Sorry to break this to you – but its not very high. When you make a cold call, here's basically how your prospect ranks YOU in his or her pecking order of priority, which determines whether or not they'll pick up the phone. From top to bottom on a scale of 1 to 10 (10 being rock-bottom) this is about how it shakes out:

1. **Company CEO/company president**
2. **The prospect's boss's boss**
3. **The prospect's boss**
4. **Their children**
5. **Family members**
6. **Friends/co-workers/friends of friends**
7. **Current vendors they like and/or perceive value**
8. **Current vendors they are indifferent about**
9. **Current vendors they don't like**
10. <u>**You**</u>**.**

Vacuum-Calling Syndrome

Sales reps today are challenged because they tend to think of their phone call (to a prospect) as if it's being made in a total vacuum - as if their phone call will be the only call their target will get all day. I know because I get a lot of feedback from frustrated sales reps asking: "Why don't they call me back? Why don't they answer the phone?"

This leads to a lot of frustration, driving sales reps to leave voice mails virtually <u>begging</u> someone to call them back. After a second or third begging voice mail from the same rep, I've actually heard demanding voice mails which go something like this: "I've left several messages and haven't heard back from you - I would *appreciate* a call back." We call this "Phone-Call-in-a-Vacuum-Syndrome" because the sales rep is acting like they are the only person calling the prospect, and that the prospect has some sort of obligation to answer or return their call. Unfortunately most sales reps think like this, even though you can see their call is at the lowest order of the prospect's pecking order of importance. We need to always remember:

- **The prospect has no idea who we are.**
- **They have many more competing priorities.**
- **We need to understand why we're so low on the prospect's priority list.**

So let's take a closer look. And as we do, <u>I'll show you how to leave begging for a call-back behind for good</u>.

Prospect Priorities Defined

Senior executives are at the top of your prospect's priority list and include the company owner, CEO and/or others at the top of the company food chain. Obviously, your prospect is going to pick up the phone immediately when they see that person calling.

Next in line is your prospect's boss's boss. If their immediate supervisor is calling, it's one thing, but if their supervisor's boss is calling, flags go up. There must be an even more significant reason for the call.

Next in line is their immediate supervisor, followed by their own kids, maybe a spouse or significant other, then friends, co-workers, friends of friends, and so forth. In other words, your prospect's priority list actually drops through seven or eight levels before they would *even think* of answering or responding to your call. And 'that's not all'! You now fall behind a list of vendors. Vendors they like and/or respect have significantly higher priority over you and your call; these are vendors that they consider critical to their business.

Next in line come vendors they know of but don't like, believe it or not, followed by vendors they know but don't care about. Yes, it's true: A vendor they're indifferent about - or even a vendor they don't like - will get their attention before you do. Why? …<u>Because they have some reason to respond</u>.

Now, here's a bit of a foreshadowing secret: One of these people may be <u>a new sales rep they've talked to before</u>, someone <u>who has built some level of credibility</u> or a rapport with them. Aha! **This is where we begin to climb the ladder.** I'll explain later.

[**Tip:** If you can <u>get referrals from any of the above</u> - referrals from any of the people we've just talked about – you can <u>instantly move up in the prospect's hierarchy of priority</u>.]

But don't feel too bad - <u>now we know why they ignore our calls.</u> Here's a behind-scenes look at *them*, as they look at *you*:

- Their phone rings.
- Their Caller ID says it's "ABC Staffing" (you).
- They think, "Who?"
- Then they think: "It's just another staffing company trying to sell me something."
- An inner voice tells them, "ABC is like all the rest."

They ignore the call, of course, and go back to whatever they were doing. Obviously, we need to take a different approach. We need to do things much differently than we did in the past.

Shotgun Burn-Out

Here's the problem: In today's relentless barrage of communication alternatives, the old "shotgun" approach to selling just isn't working any more. Most sales people are stuck shooting aimlessly hoping they hit something. They end up burning themselves out as they make a bunch of cold calls and haphazard follow-ups, all with unrealistic expectations of what it takes to be truly successful.

To make things worse, sales managers continue to tell them to do these things, driving them to make "as many calls as possible" while hoping something good will happen. Tied to the traditional shotgun approach with frustration mounting, we can't stay on top of all our prospects and effectively maximize our opportunities. Even more problematic, given the realities of a communications revolution it has become <u>extremely difficult</u> to reach out to prospects with the kind of variable frequency necessary…without having some kind of controlled structure wrapped around the selling process.

Now don't get me wrong – I am not telling you to stop making phone calls. Phone calls are and will continue to be one of the most effective sales activities we can do. But it needs to be targeted and consistent, and supported by other sales activities to be successful today and in the future. A <u>structured sales process gives us a consistent, controllable roadmap</u> designed to move our prospects through the selling process to close. That's why the structured sales process has become such an integral part of the way top producers do business today.

Structured Simplicity

Let's talk about some of the higher levels of the sales process, which are key elements to be addressed in detail in this book. But rest easy, it's all about keeping things simple, all about taking a load off instead of adding to it.

Structure is at the center of the matrix, of course. Structure will keep you focused, positive and moving forward. Here, we're talking about a simple, proven, repeatable sales process. Again, simplicity is at the heart of it all. In fact, everything I do, when it comes to sales and sale management, is simple by design. This is because anything 'complicated' will eventually be abandoned by sales people immersed in a fast-paced, competitive selling environment.

Simple means "power" with so many business models, as you will discover while tracking the powerful impact of my structured sales process, and see how easy it is to use. My process has been streamlined so that the same, user-friendly methods can be used repeatedly, and effectively, over and over again.

The Six Proven Steps to

Sales Power

My sales process I address throughout this book is broken into six proven steps. Here they are:

Step 1: Identify Suspect Companies and Contacts. We'll get into more detail of what "Suspects" are, but for now, know that Suspects are basically <u>unqualified prospects</u>. I'm going to show you how to go out and find your suspects, how to prequalify them, and how to identify different types of contacts in suspect companies.

Step 2: Implement a 12-Touch, 10-Week Sales Contact Schedule (to be covered in upcoming chapters). We'll go through it in detail as I explain why we need to hit our suspects enough times to build credibility and familiarity, while getting our message through. When you ultimately make contact in the right way, you already will have established a level of credibility that will put you higher up on your suspect's priority list.

Step 3: Qualify your Suspects to Turn them into Prospects and "Targets." As you qualify, you will also "disqualify" your suspects, as you move them into, or out of, the 10-week sales process. No more begging. Just qualifying and disqualifying to maximize *your* goals.

Step 4: Add Opportunities from the Process to a Streamlined Sales Pipeline. This allows us to actually manage the companies and contacts in our sales process. As we do, we pay close attention to our opportunities as we follow a defined sales pipeline.

Step 5: Work Opportunities Through Your Pipeline Stages. I will define those Pipeline Stages in more detail, showing their importance in how you determine which stage a prospect falls into, and how we finally close them out as wins and losses.

Step 6: Continue Feeding Suspects into the Structured Sales Process. Keep adding new suspects and run them through the structured sales process. This is vital. It actually creates the core of a self-perpetuating, suspect-development cycle that we continue to run through the process…as we disqualify and qualify suspects, while replacing them with other suspects.

If it sounds complicated, trust me, it isn't. It's just a matter of making a few, simple changes in the way we do business. **Think of the structured sales process as a circular flow of water through a pool.** Our suspects simply flow through a basically mechanized 10-week process as we qualify some/disqualify others, while adding qualified opportunities to our "pipeline." Then it's time to close out wins and losses, and get paid…<u>as we continuously refresh the 10-week sales process with new suspects</u>. That's the key. Look at the entire process like recirculating fresh water through a pool. Your business never goes stagnant. And you avoid the "roller-coaster" effect to your sales pipeline that most sales people experience over and over.

Six Moves to Master 'Chess' in Sales

The point I want to make is that my 10-week program is only part of the whole. The entire system is really a Six Point Process of **Selling as a Game of Chess**:

The Six-Step Sales Process

Get off the sales rollercoaster

We've talked about the basics and importance of the structured sales process. If you've been in sales for any length of time, you've probably experienced what we call the "sales rollercoaster" – those peaks and valleys that come from inconsistent prospecting activity. This happens when we do a bunch of prospecting activity, get some hits, work them through the sales process, and close the deals out as one or lost. All the while, we stop prospecting. So once we move these opportunities through to conclusion, we have to start all over again. Many sales professionals have hit sustained and sometimes devastating income droughts because of this. Well, I'm about to demonstrate a simple method that will not only grow your productivity and efficiency, it will close those dreaded gaps while increasing a steady flow of income. This is how top producers become so successful, and our process teaches exactly how to do this.

Most retirement planners point to one important fact: having a reliable, consistent income is more valuable in the long-run than getting a big windfall in the stock market. Translated to sales production, I'm going to show you how to get income consistency while growing your production exponentially, and in some cases explosively. All you need is an open mind, persistence, and a modest commitment of time.

My process isn't about a radical change to sales. It's about making simple, lasting changes that drive performance and reward you exponentially.

Re-Thinking the Way We Think

One of the keys to improving your sales results is to step back and re-think normal human behavior. For decades, the way we've been taught to sell really goes against our nature as human beings. It's more important than ever to see old selling tactics as they truly are: we call people up, interrupt their day, and immediately try to convince them to give us an appointment. If it works (which it rarely does), we then get in front of them and try to get them to do business with us on the first try. There are several problems with this approach: First, we are utilizing tactics on our prospects that we HATE when they are used on us. And, <u>we are trying to force our pace, not theirs</u>. It's like aggressively trying to get someone to marry us before they even know our name. We instead trigger their defenses, turning them off to us, forcing them more often than not to say "No."

'Evolution' not Revolution

I'm not asking you to upend everything you know and adopt some 'revolutionary' new selling miracle. I'm asking you to evolve in order to work with the realities of selling today.

We've rolled out my evolutionary approach for hundreds of staffing sales people, from veterans to rookies. Some are true sales veterans who have implemented this process, seen astounding results, and have come back to us with overwhelmingly positive feedback. We're talking about people who have been in staffing industry sales for over 20, sometimes 30 years. Others have been brand new to the industry, and we were able to kick-start their careers with with a significantly reduced ramp-up period and similarly explosive results.

Giving Reps "A *Real* Reason" to Connect

Feedback has been consistent and conclusive: our structured process makes selling so much easier because people suddenly feel like they "have a real reason" to make that contact.

Veteran sales people say it also gives them the structure to know exactly what to do next. It eliminates the old "bogged down" spinning-our-wheels kind of feeling. It alleviates the uneasy sense that we may not be doing the right things at the right time, leaving us vulnerable to those dreaded droughts and gaps in production. So, without turning people into mechanical droids, our process creates an energizing, humanizing structure, one that has inspired countless sales professionals to proclaim they will "never sell another way again." <u>Our process is just that transformative</u>.

When some of our now successful sales reps first came to us, they had no prospects, no opportunities in their pipeline, no targets. But after just a few months of utilizing the process, they quickly progressed from having zero opportunities to having full pipelines, leading to multiple new clients - all generating impressive revenue and, ultimately, substantial commissions.

They've also learned to adopt a realistic perspective. Without beating themselves up, they now understand that the vast majority of suspects and prospects will not turn into clients. But they also see that only a small fraction of prospects are needed to closed deals and become successful. With that in mind, you will find that our structured sales process becomes easier by-the-day to manage and maintain as you enjoy an astounding increase in your results.

Evolve Your Approach

If you're a bit skeptical about new things (and you're not alone), I'm not asking you to completely change the way you've been doing business. We're just talking about adding structure to what you do well, while adopting new components and perspectives to make those activities more effective. And when I say "effective," I'm talking about results. We've seen the results over and over again. Regardless of where they were when they began our program, the sales professionals that have embraced this process have greatly improved their productivity. They have learned how to develop and land significantly more deals.

That said, we're ready to move on to the next chapter. In the upcoming pages, I am going to ask you to suspend your preconceptions about 'sales' in general. I want you to examine the way you look at selling, and as you do, I want you to adopt a new goal: I want you to change the way you think about your prospects. And as we progress through the following pages, I believe that you will discover exciting new concepts that will grow results in other ways - just by making a few, simple alterations in how you approach the playing field.

You are going to be challenged to make a fundamental shift in your sales mindset. If you can make the change and process the fundamental concepts I'm about to introduce in the next chapter, I'm confident you will gain a new sense of ease and comfort in everything you do.

No More Self-Abuse

You are about to abandon the worn-out, self-punishing concepts associated with unrealistic expectations, which does little more than create unnecessary stress and burnout. The notorious old syndrome of self-abuse ultimately feeds a sense of failure rather than sparking performance.

So, the next chapter will open the door to a more productive new perspective.

- **I'm going to alter the way you approach the world of selling.**
- **I will help you change the way you look at, and approach prospects.**

- **I will show you new ways to manage your sales cycle.**

To get there, we need to recognize that we have been driven by antiquated attitudes and methodologies. Those outdated "strategies" have, in fact, led many people in the wrong direction, actually *reducing* their effectiveness over time. Have you have ever felt this way? My guess is you have, and if so, you are not alone. In fact, this is what inspired me to develop our structured sales process.

Now it's your turn. Isn't it about time to get away from "the wall" and breathe more easily? As I show you how to apply our methodology to your evolved new thought processes, you will be able to visualize a more consistent, dependable and structured way of making sales. In a word, "consistency" is about to become a freshly operative term for some people.

While enjoying a dramatic rise in closed deals, you will also find yourself simultaneously regenerating new potential sales, eliminating those financially crippling gaps between closed deals and commissions – or what we call the "sales rollercoaster."

...On to the gaming table, where we will discover how to "**think chess, not war**."

CHAPTER TWO

'Selling' Is a Game of Chess

Most sales reps are taught to approach sales as individual, or groups of unrelated transactions. I call it "thinking transactional," as in: one interaction = one transaction. We get all pumped up for that initial assault, that win or lose, do or die sales pitch. If the initial assault fails, many sales reps are quick to abandon the opportunity and move on to the next lead. I know this, I've seen it time and again, and early in my career I felt it too.

First, we need to drop the traditional pass-or-fail sales mentality. This chapter is all about re-thinking the way we approach selling.

Chess Not War

From here on out, I want you to approach sales as a game of chess, not war. Think about the card game known as *War*, where two opponents face each other, throw down a card, and the high card wins. It's a very 'transactional' game with a winner and loser every time. That's how most sales people are trained to approach sales calls. The sales rep faces the prospect, makes an all-out pitch to get that appointment or an order, the prospect either submits and says Yes, or resists and says No.

Whenever we ask sales reps to name their number-one goal when cold calling, almost every single time they'll answer: "Get an appointment, or get an order." When making a phone call, anything less than an appointment or job order is considered a failure –we lost the game.

Now you can see why I call this kind of approach very "transactional" in nature. It's a one-time, do-or-die, singular-event interaction, one in which we either win or lose. With this type of approach to sales, the word "No" from a prospect tends to be final (and "No" can be a literal one, or more commonly just a lack of responsiveness to our calls and emails). Success means, "Yes, I got an appointment/I got an order." Failure is everything else.

We run into several problems with the *War* approach – the biggest being that prospects no longer make decisions this way. They all want more information, more detail. They need to feel as if they've looked at every angle before they'll even start to make a decision. And information to make decisions is more plentiful than ever before with the internet and social media at their fingertips. In staffing, prospects are bombarded with sales reps calling to make transactional-style pitches for business. Here's what happens…

How to Set Yourself Up for Failure

When our definition of success is to get an appointment or order on the first call, we set ourselves up for disappointment. It's a completely unrealistic expectation. First off, we aren't giving the prospect enough time to consider if they *want* to spend their limited time with us - in person, in a face-to-face appointment. The 'one-call, one-time' approach almost certainly *will not* get orders on a very first cold call. Why? … Because they know nothing about us, and usually we sound like every other staffing sales rep that calls on them every day. So, when we approach sales as a transactional game of war, what we're really doing is setting ourselves up for failure.

We need to understand that other positive outcomes are possible, and there *should be* other outcomes. For example, even leaving a series of voice mails can have positive outcomes if we take the right approach. So, instead of looking at sales activities as individual events, we need to see them as building blocks, each building on an earlier attempt. When we do that, we approach the prospect differently. It will come across loud and clear in what you say, and how you say it. Shove ourselves into a do-or-die, one-time "encounter" and we might sound pushy, edgy, even desperate - because we know we probably have only one chance to get an appointment with a contact.

Relax. Play Chess. Pace Your Moves.

By utilizing a well-structured, multi-step process, it allows us to approach that phone call in a much more relaxed and confident manner. We are positioning ourselves to go farther down the pathway to an actual relationship, without the artificial, self-imposed stress of needing an appointment. In the game of chess, we know we can't win the game in one or two moves, but we can (and should) set ourselves up for the next move. When you think about sales as a game of chess, you think of selling in much the same way.

All you really do at the beginning of a chess game is one, simple thing: you set yourself up for the next move. When you get really good at chess, you learn to think three moves ahead, then five, then 10 or even 15 moves down the road. That's how you win the game in the end.

This is how we need to approach sales. We need to look at our very first interaction with them as a mere building block to additional steps. When we think of sales as a game of chess, we know it's rare to land deals or get appointments on the first call. In fact, I instruct sales reps I train and coach to <u>not even try</u> to get an appointment on the first call! Of course, if the opportunity naturally presents itself to get an appointment during the first call, you take it. Just don't go in with that objective. Human beings (which is what our prospects are) are wary; they sense intentions and are quick to put up barriers. Instead, you focus on accomplishing three things in every call:

- Start to build **rapport**
- Establish some **credibility**
- Begin creating interest through **differentiating** yourself

If your first contact naturally leads to a deeper conversation on the first call, that's great. If an even deeper conversation leads to an appointment, that's even better. But don't look for that at first. We've found that when we take the pressure off the sales people, when we tell them NOT to try to get that appointment on the first call, here's what tends to happen:

- **They end up having much more 'natural' conversations with the prospect**
- **Prospects relax and let down their guard**
- **They end up having much more 'meaningful' conversations**
- **They actually get *more* appointments!**

This is why we approach sales as a game of chess, not war. In fact, this reflects an ancient method of doing business in Asia called "The Legend of the Thirteen Cups." When pursuing a business or strategic goal, students were taught to expect to share a cup of tea with a prospect during the first meeting and to do the same during 12 subsequent meetings. That was the proper protocol to be expected before an agreement would be reached. While it might seem charmingly time-consuming and out of touch today, it isn't. It says volumes about the establishment of credibility and trust...which takes time. Our structured process will show you how to pace your moves. Chess is an ancient game in which strategic victory was achieved after the planning of multiple moves... over time. Have we changed that much as human beings? Our findings show that we haven't change all that much at all.

We've developed our 10-week, 12-step contact schedule based on the Chess Master concept. It's really about acknowledging that sales is a process, and positioning ourselves for the NEXT step without setting unrealistic expectations for ourselves, or for the actions of our prospect. What we're really trying to do from the very <u>first</u> interaction, is to introduce what we do <u>differently</u> than others in our industry and start to build some interest, and over time, demand.

This allows us to put a critical piece into play on the chess board, our....

...Compelling Value Proposition

The biggest challenge we have in the staffing industry – in most industries, really – is that when we reach out to pitch a product or service, we all sound the same. A lot of people accordingly say that the staffing industry has been commoditized because of a lack of discernable differences between companies. Again, everybody sounds the same.

When asked what makes their staffing firm different, nearly every sales rep answers with a version of "quality": the "quality" of our placements, the "quality" of our staff, and/or the "quality" of our customer service. Our prospects and clients consider the word "quality" to be as worn and clichéd as words like "strategy" and "synergy."

I personally learned this the hard way early in my staffing sales career. I had the opportunity to bid on a fairly large staffing user and was asked to come in to present. I must have been the 5th or 6th staffing firm that presented that day. The prospect asked me the classic question "what makes you different than the other staffing firms that presented today?" And I, of course, started in on the classic answer: "Well, it's the quality of our placements and internal staff...."

Before I could finish my response (which I'm not sure even I believed), the prospect started laughing. When I asked him what was funny, he said something that changed my entire approach to sales, for the better.

"I'm sorry," the prospect said, "I shouldn't have laughed. But when you start in the staffing industry, do they *issue you a book* that tells you how to answer that question? Because every one of you has answered it the **same exact way**!"

So, when we reach out to our suspects, how can we expect them to differentiate between us when we aren't helping them see the difference?

With this approach, we leave them the only remaining differentiator: price...or a sales rep who can bug them repeatedly without turning them off altogether – good luck playing *that* game.

That's why we've become so commoditized. That's why it has become so difficult for us to get appointments and have conversations with companies. It's not that they don't need our services. It's because they get bombarded by so many staffing companies that sound so much alike. They have no time to look at the background of everyone coming through the door, and that leaves only one alternative for success:

It is absolutely crucial to your success that you develop a compelling "Value Proposition." You must show the <u>unique value </u>your company offers its customers.

Two important points form this powerful equation and make it resonate with prospects. First, you must <u>demonstrate why you are "unique."</u> Second, you need to <u>show why you are "valuable."</u> We need to <u>show both "value" and "uniqueness."</u> If we offer value, for example, without being unique, we still haven't been able to differentiate ourselves from the pack. And vice versa.

Unique/Value Differentiators

Here's an example: When I ask staffing companies to identify things that make them unique – in many cases they talk about their screening process, particularly background checks and drug screens. But here's the problem: screening isn't unique! It is widely offered in our industry. And while there certainly is *value* in screening, it lacks uniqueness, and therefore *can't* be a differentiator. Conversely, if you're offering something that is unique *but <u>lacks perceived value</u>* in the eyes of the prospect, then it's not a value proposition and you lose the attention of your prospect. Ever heard someone say, "I watched his/her eyes glaze over" when commiserating about a failed pitch? This happens all the time when a prospect <u>hears no value</u> in a proposal.

As an example, early on in my career and for a large national staffing firm, we had just come out with a new client portal. This was cutting edge for the time. We were one of the early companies to come out with an online website that would allow the client to get online and actually order contract employees. At the same time, they could also pull some near-real-time reports – how awesome was that!? We thought it was great technology, we knew it was unique, and we were sure it would provide a lot of value to customers and prospects. So, we started to go out and sell it, showing how it made us different, showing that they would be able to run reports anytime on all sorts of different topics. I would proudly run a demonstration and then I'd ask them what they thought.

I was surprised by the answer. They would shake their heads and say, "Well, that's great but we want YOU to run the reports." In other words, it was *unique* but to them it lacked *value* because they had no interest in actually working with it themselves. They considered it something we were supposed to do as part of our service. So, fantastic as we thought it was, it wasn't a differentiator. It lacked a strong Value Proposition.

Building a Value Proposition

To build a strong Value Proposition, we first need to understand our competition. It is critical that we conduct ongoing research to fully <u>understand the strengths and weaknesses of our competitors</u>. This is key. Never make assumptions. When I was in sales for a staffing firm, I had major competitors in my market, and I thought I knew their strengths and weaknesses. But later, when I went into consulting, I ultimately wound up with some of my old competitors as clients. I was finally able to see what they were about, what they did well, what their challenges really were. What a revelation! I realized that, as their competitor I had been focusing on defining their weaknesses…without looking more closely at their strengths. (and about half the time I was wrong about their weaknesses too)

In other words, when I had been competing with that company, I'd really had no clue. I was completely wrong about what they were good at versus what they weren't. Therefore, the sales strategy I'd once used to compete with them was based on misconceptions. In other words, I had never taken the time to research and understand their strengths and weaknesses.

Once we understand our competition's strengths and weaknesses, we need to look at what makes **us** better and different. Only then can we talk about our differentiators with a feeling of *confidence* and *authority*. Even more important is our ability to QUANTIFY what makes us better and different. Can we actually show it? Can we really talk about how our service beats theirs with confidence and authority? We can shout all day about our "great" customer service, but trust me, staffing companies with the world's worst customer service are running around bragging about their great customer service too. So, it all begins to fall on deaf ears. Prospects have been burned. They know everyone is going to brag about their customer service, screening, internal team, etc.

Break Out with Differentiators

When we can talk about our "great" customer service AND back it up with, for example, a couple of awards (such as Inavero's Best of Staffing), that's what I mean by quantification. Now, let's add a few reinforcing client testimonials. Now we are providing proof. They quantify our claims and separate us from the rest – especially from those who don't quantify (which is just about every other staffing firm).

Think about how you make a major purchase (anything over $100 or so). Do you just run out and buy it? Well, you might if it's an emergency purchase, like a blown tire that needs replaced or a dishwasher that is flooding your kitchen. But in most cases, we do our research. We go to formal product reviewers like Consumer Reports and Angie's List. We look at online customer reviews. We ask our friends in person and on social media. Essentially, we are looking for proof to support our purchasing decision.

This reflects a point I made in the previous chapter, when I talked about the different ways people buy. Just as we require independent support that we are making a wise purchase, so do our prospects. When we can provide proof such as testimonials, awards, and case studies, it helps a prospect feel more comfortable with the decision to continue to talk to us.

Other ways to quantify are with metrics, meaning different measurements. Metrics include time to fill, turnover, and conversion rates – can we quantifiably show, for instance, that our turnover rates are lower than the competition?

Search for Clues

Look to data, reports, and surveys done by industry experts, including organizations such as the American Staffing Association, the National Association of Personnel Services, Staffing Industry Analysts, and major industry suppliers. You will find a variety of relevant, timely information to help benchmark your organization and reinforce your differentiators.

Websites such as Glassdoor, Google, and Facebook are great for finding reviews about your competitors and prospects. These are often posted by employees offering feedback about that company, with inside information about leadership and, in many cases, you get great insight into what's going on inside the organization itself. A word of warning: take what you read with a grain of salt because you tend to get feedback from complainers. But you can read between the lines, look for common themes, and still put your finger on the pulse of that company.

You can also look within your own company, among **candidates and contract employees** coming through the door who have experience working with your competition. Ask them what's good and bad about the other staffing firms they have worked with.

Adding Credibility

Now let's think about things that give us additional credibility, including **memberships** with associations valued by the prospect, and our **experience,** either individually or as a company. For example, I work with a health care staffing company as a client that happens to be owned and operated by a registered nurse. This makes her and her company more credible. I have several clients that can say that all their employees have industry certification, which gives them added credibility because it shows that they are truly professionals committed to the industry, and that they have a greater understanding of employment law.

We also must think about what's important to the client, because ultimately this is about "perceived" value, not just value. It all comes down to one question: does the client find value in what we are offering? Value can be determined simply by asking existing customers why they work with us. So, if we think something about our company makes us different, let's see if our customers agree. Then let's ask if this difference is important to them.

We also learn from talking to prospects who decide <u>not</u> to select us. Whenever possible, we should **conduct exit interviews** and ask them what happened. As painful as this may be, we want to understand their perception of value, which may include things we don't offer…or maybe even things we have, but *failed to emphasize*.

In the end, knowledge is power. We need to understand what's important to the prospect, what we do better than our competitors, and how we can back it up with proof. Otherwise it's just assumptions and lip service.

Honing Your Value Proposition

Once you create a Value Proposition, you need to boil it down and make it succinct for your presentation. Start with an introductory sentence or two and emphasize it with two to four bullet points. Your bullet points should focus on why you're different and should emphasize value to the client. Your value proposition statement is then used as the "source code" for all your marketing communication, from your elevator pitch, to your website, to social media, presentations, and proposals.

Then it's up to you to own your value prop. Make it so ingrained in your messaging that it's automatic. For example, let's say you're placed on hold by a receptionist and someone high up in the company suddenly clicks into the line by mistake. You now have 10 seconds to introduce yourself. Be ready. Write it down in advance, boil it down, practice and stick to it. Say it to the mirror, to your spouse, to a colleague. Leave yourself and/or your colleagues voice mails. Look at your dog and try it out (pretty funny depending on the dog). Make it work. Make it memorable. Make it yours.

Here's the point: you can leave a minute-long voice mail, even a two-minute voice mail if you can capture their interest in the first 10 to 15 seconds. I've talked to many decision makers including owners, company presidents, CEOs, division managers - you name it - and I've asked this question: "If a sales person catches your interest at the beginning of a voice mail, will you listen to a longer voice mail?"

Every single time they say, "Yes, absolutely."

Think about newspaper headlines and lead paragraphs in magazine articles. Listen to compelling little headlines announced by news anchors at the top of a broadcast. What do they have in common? They hint at arresting news, don't they? We'll get into this in depth in upcoming chapters of this book, and we go even deeper into other messaging techniques in our training classes and seminars. For now, **practice, condense, and *be prepared***. Power-up your messaging for voice mails, emails, a 15-second elevator chat, a brief encounter at lunch or during a networking event. Think about everything as a potential opportunity.

Make Your Final Moves Count

In this chapter I haven't tried to change absolutely everything you do. I've simply tried to change the way you think about the selling process. Call it chess, call it the Legend of the 13 Cups, either way, we're going to take the pressure off that very first cold call. When you're finished with this book, you will be able to relax if your suspect is called away from the phone, or finds an arbitrary reason to end the call. I am going to show you how to make it part of an ongoing process of contacts that will turn things around.

I will then show you how to take those moments and change the outcome of every call you make, from this point forward. I will show you how to play the game of sales like chess, just by planning a few moves ahead.

What it really boils down to is this: when you approach sales as a game of chess, you take more control of human interactions because, now, you're dealing with prospects as people - not one-shot leads. My system lets you to approach the sales process as a developing relationship because you utilize multiple steps in a methodical process. You no longer feel pressured to treat every contact as a do-or-die transactional encounter. You will no longer generate a tense, adversarial situation in which you're trying to just get in, get out, and chalk up an encounter as a success or failure.

<u>Your</u> Stress Reduction Reduces <u>Their</u> Defensiveness

If you can adopt this philosophy it will not only reduce your stress level, your reduced stress level will lower the defenses of your prospect. You're no longer pushing a one-time, 30-second phone pitch. You will approach that call differently than most other sales people in our industry, which ultimately will lead to more success, more appointments and – just as important - stronger relationships (leading to referrals, testimonials and more).

Follow the methods in this book and suddenly you will be able to approach that prospect from **a** more **consultative standpoint**, rather than taking on the role of someone trying to just sell a product or service. Now you're advising and guiding, you're offering help and insight, all without jumping straight into a pitch. You will abandon that defensive sense of entitlement some sales people adopt when their prospect picks up the phone. You will no longer push for the make-or-break. Now, you're letting a relationship evolve, and with that evolution comes unexpected opportunities. These include further insight into other opportunities within that organization, referrals beyond the company...the sky's the limit when you know how to play the game!

CHAPTER THREE

Suspects, Prospects and Targets – A Game of Finesse

In this chapter, we're going to look at the importance of differentiating the different types of prospects. During your approach, each separate group – suspects, prospects or targets – will require a separate set of developmental steps.

In the next few pages, we will also go in-depth to identify creative ways to find contact information, while providing tips on how to avoid making critical gaffs when getting in touch with prospects.

But first, you need to closely study the three major delineations covered in this chapter, those being suspects, prospects and targets. Well-defined delineations are important components of a Structured Sales Process and once identified, they will work non-stop for you. They will increase your production exponentially. They will close those occasionally troublesome income gaps faced by many sales people.

After years in sales, I've been exposed to most, if not all, of the top sales methodologies. And most of them are great. The problem is that these processes almost always focus on what to do *after* you've gotten your foot in the door. But where most sales reps struggle is the part of the sales process *before* there is an opportunity. It doesn't matter how well I manage opportunities if I don't have any opportunities.

So, what we are going to focus on in this section is that very thing – How do I even get my foot in the door? To begin the process, we first want to identify what we refer to as "suspects." Let's start right here:

Suspects

"Suspects" can refer to either companies or contacts that are 'suspected' of utilizing staffing. But suspects have not yet been "qualified" as actual prospects.

Qualification is part of the process and we'll get to that in moment. But first, we need to think of suspects as those entities having company or department characteristics very similar to what we already have as staffing clients. A suspect differs in that it has not yet been fully vetted out; we probably haven't even talked to anyone in the suspect company or department, for example. We still don't know whether or not they actually utilize staffing - maybe due to a lack of general market knowledge - or maybe we've never spoken to someone from this particular company. That's why we call them "suspects."

Once we've identified them as suspects, we begin the process of qualifying (and disqualifying) to 'prospect' status. During this period of the process – we call it the "Pre-Pipeline" process – we engage in something I like to call "Focused Prospecting." Instead of just calling up a bunch of companies, we <u>focus on the characteristics</u> of suspects worth pursuing. To do that, we ask ourselves a few questions about potential suspects;

- **Do they share similar characteristics to companies that use staffing?**
- **Do they have seasonality or project work that would necessitate contract staff ?**
- **Are they in high-turnover areas or skill sets?**
- **Do they have extremely difficult positions to fill? (software developers, registered nurses, skilled trades, etc.)**
- **Are they in an industry that typically utilizes contract staffing? (third-party logistics, manufacturing, corporate offices, software development, etc.)**

Depending upon the staffing vertical, the characteristics listed above would help you identify potential companies or departments as suspects. Once we identify our suspects, then we're ready to put them through our 10-week prospecting process. And as we do, we will either qualify or disqualify them as potential prospects. In other words, while the next step is to take them to "prospect" status, some won't cut it. They won't make it through our qualification process, and that's ok, because it just further hones our focus on those most likely to buy our services.

Prospects

Prospects are essentially companies or contacts that we know utilize staffing, or at least are open to it. They made it through our suspect qualification process, we now know they need staffing, but we haven't been able to have conversations that would lead to potential opportunities. By the way, these may be companies we know our competitors are working with; they may be companies our contract employees have talked about; or, we simply know about the company having been in the market for a period of time. These are prospects.

Targets

Once we've had conversations with a prospect and the door opens – even slightly - to their possible utilization of our services, that prospect becomes a target. Targets are the best few companies or contacts in our pipeline offering tangible opportunities. Similar to suspects and prospects but with a higher probability of success, a target can be a company, department or contact.

This is where things get interesting because you could have, say, an overall target company with a client in one department while having suspects and prospects in other areas of the same company. You might actually have all four categories within one company: clients, suspects, prospects and targets. For example, let's say you work with a large organization doing business in their call center. They also utilize staffing in their warehouse, but you haven't been able to convince them to talk with you yet. You think they use contractors in their IT department, but haven't talked with anyone. And at the same time, you are in conversations with their accounting department about some openings they may give you to work on.

In this case, the call center would be your client, the warehouse is a prospect, the IT department would be a suspect, and the accounting department would be considered a target. This may seem unlikely, but in larger organizations it is not only likely, but a sign of healthy account penetration. All kinds of interconnecting opportunities are going to develop within your pipeline when you play the game this way. Obviously, you're going to be _way ahead_ of transactional people going for the immediate sale or appointment.

Built-In Time Management

So, that's the overall concept of suspects, prospects and targets. Now let's talk about time management.

This is where so many sales reps trip themselves up, because they lose track of the kind of efficient scheduling only a structured sales process can secure. If we're always in a race with ourselves to call on new companies and contacts, we tend to throw out too wide of a net. When that happens – and lot of sales reps fall into this – they just keep going and going, without really going anywhere. They always seem to be in motion without scratching the surface. Other sales reps have the opposite problem – they cast too narrow of a net and fail to go after enough companies and contacts. This is why I began to develop the goal-based process for a more complete development of suspects, prospects and targets.

So, what does this process look like in real-time for the average sales rep? First, I recommend a healthy pre-pipeline consists of_ about 300 suspects, 100 prospects and 25 to 30 targets_. This might sound like a tall order in itself, but think about it: if you put yourself to the task, you could probably generate 300 suspects in a few hours.

After generating 300 suspects, you begin to process them into prospects and targets…as you constantly replenish new suspects into your pipeline. So, it's a little like a perpetual motion machine. Once you get it going and feed it on a regular basis, it seems as if it begins to run itself as you put your suspects, prospects and targets through the process to become clients. As we mentioned earlier, this allows us to avoid the sales rollercoaster almost all sales reps experience at some point in their careers.

The nature of the market also has a place on our chess board. Mature markets obviously differ from cold markets. If you're jumping into a cold market, you'll have a lot more suspects. If you're replacing another sales rep that has been there awhile, or if you've been in a market for a period of time, you would be in a more mature market with more prospects because much of the vetting has already been done. The reason why we set goals for suspects, prospects, and targets is so we have a balanced approach to prospecting, casting the right size net to stay focused without putting too many eggs in one basket.

"We've Never Thought This way"

When I start to sit down and go through an actual structured process, most sales reps say, "We've never thought this way, we've never been taught this way." Like most of us, they started out with the old shotgun approach because that's what they were taught. That's what I did when I started out because I didn't know any better.

My process differentiates radically from other sales books and training programs. As I said in the beginning of this book, that stuff is fine once you have your foot in the door, but what about generating the first appointment? Well, I'm about to show you how to do it with such consistency, you'll wonder why you ever prospected any other way.

So how do we begin at the very beginning? How do we first begin to identify the Suspects that feed our structured pipeline? Here's how:

Secrets to "Suspect" Identification

While there are hundreds of different ways to identify suspects, I tell sales reps to focus primarily on two areas.

A.) You can get all the suspects you need with an **Advanced Search** through **LinkedIn**, which would be focused on the criteria we've talked about. You may already use LinkedIn, but let's look at a couple of ways to ramp it up a notch: first, you want to focus on what the suspect should look like; once you get the results you're looking for, save that search and **run a contact search** in LinkedIn. Then, set it up to receive **daily and weekly alerts** to feed you a continuous flow of leads. With those in motion, we no longer need to race after traditional "prospecting" activities.

To summarize:

- **Run an advanced search with your contact criteria**
- **Save the Search**
- **Receive daily/weekly email alerts**

Note: LinkedIn is continually changing the features available to users based on the free or premium account they have. The process described above is available to Sales Navigator users. You can still run searches with a free or lower-level premium account, but the functionality is limited.

B.) Go to **Indeed.com**, the world's largest job board aggregator. Doing searches on Indeed is great because, while it has its own postings, it also pulls jobs from other job boards and company websites. You can see how easy it is to turn it all around: it's a one-stop search if you're looking for a job, of course, but you can also use it to prospect because **it reveals companies posting open positions**. In short, when we see who's looking for positions, we also know **who might utilize staffing**.

If you think about it, we are in the unique and enviable position of being one of the only industries where **our prospects actually advertise their need for our services**!

More Suspect-Searching Tools

Other job boards are out there and ripe for the use of sales reps in the staffing industry. Every one of them can be tapped to quickly and efficiently to stock your pool of Suspects. These important sources will also help you re-fill your Suspect Pool again and again, like fresh-water streaming into a pond, to keep it from going stagnant.

Suspect-refilling streams include **CareerBuilder, Monster, and niche job boards**. Online contact databases include Data.com, **Hoovers**, **Harris**, and **InfoUSA.** Each has its own way of tracking and cataloguing data, but it can be well worth the effort to set up similar search and alert functions through these sites.

Offline Sources

Other resources can be just as valuable, including annual and semi-annual Book of Lists published by city "**business journals.**" These tightly focused executive newspapers can be found in downtown/high-density employment areas around most major cities (i.e., Atlanta Business Chronicle, Houston Business Chronicle, Denver Business Journal). Their Book of Lists are chock-full of company/employment info, employment/hiring statistics, departments and more. And almost all of them have online resources that you can subscribe to and receive daily or weekly email alerts for free.

Candidate resumes and references can also be helpful, especially when working with contract employees. In many cases, candidate resumes list past **contract assignments** and even their **hiring managers**. Finally, we can tap into the other social media resources including **Twitter, Google+, and Facebook**. Use these valuable, free resources as a long-term source of fresh Suspect information because, once in motion, your Suspects are constantly qualified/disqualified as Prospects, then Targets and, finally Clients. For you, your suspect flow never stops if you keep refilling the pond.

I've given you a quick rundown of Suspect-generating shortcuts, more of which you will find in our on-site/online seminars and webinars – and all of which are keyed to the processes in this book - but in even more detail. When we began looking at ways to generate Suspects, earlier in this book, the idea of coming up with 300 in a single day might have sounded like a tall order. By now, however, I think you can see how easy it really is and how sustainable it can be with fairly minimal effort.

Don't Forget to Network, Network…Network!

Now it's back to the "tried and true," meaning: network, network… network! Networking may be part of your DNA, but we also need to reach out beyond our respective industry mixers and events. Networking is also about getting out and going to **associations where your suspects and prospects are members** – HR associations, manufacturing and IT associations, accounting and finance associations, health care organizations and associations. Just about every industry and avocation has an association, so if an organization fits your Suspect identity, join it (with a couple of cautionary caveats I'll talk about shortly).

Hunting Emails: Reaching In to Reach Out

Next, we need to work on gathering contact information. We're going to be mailing, emailing and calling people. For that, we need their mailing addresses, which tend to be the easiest to get. Then we'll be looking for emails, which can be some of the toughest information to get. After that, we'll get phone numbers, which usually come with emails (or we just call the main number and follow the prompts).

While finding a mailing address is as easy as looking at their web site in the contact us section, email-locating techniques are where we really want to focus, and I have a few methods that have worked well for us.

One of the easiest email-locating tools is a web site called **Hunter (hunter.io)**. This handy site offers several services, including an email verifier, and a company email search that allows you to identify the email naming convention for a specific company.

Places like **LinkedIn** take a little more time and may include an email in the bio, especially if you're targeting sales or public relations people (who tend to list their emails). **ContactOut** and Lusha are other great tools to use with LinkedIn. Both provide a Google Chrome plug-in that when viewing a LinkedIn profile, will search the internet for any email addresses, phone numbers, and social media handles. They have both free or trial subscriptions, as well as paid options. Data.com Connect is another great source of suspect contact information, and can be free if you are willing to share your contact list (or at least part of it) with the community.

Another approach is to search other employees of the suspect's company on LinkedIn, where key emails may be found. Sales people, recruiters, public and media relations professionals all are more likely to share their contact information on their LinkedIn profile. This usually reveals the company's email-naming convention formula, and you can go from there to find suspect emails.

When targeting higher-level executives, in some cases they'll show up among a board-of-directors, or as volunteers for non-profit organizations, both of which may list their email addresses. Then, of course, you can search email addresses on **Google**, although it takes longer and gets mixed results. (I'd rather forego Google, just go to a company web site and start digging.)

Trade Associations: Cautionary Caveat

As I said before, joining trade associations can be great for hunting suspects. Just join a **trade association** that would include your suspect organization. In human resource associations, for example, once you become a member you typically have access to their member directory, which contains emails and direct-line phone numbers. But be careful. Utilizing association information can be tricky.

- **Most associations prohibit direct solicitations from the member directory**
- **Don't go through the directory telling everybody you're a member**
- **Don't contact all members announcing that you're calling everyone in the directory**

I'll tell you why in a moment, as we discuss more subtle ways to use that information in the upcoming pages of this book.

(Big) Mistakes to Avoid

Now for those Cautionary Caveats, meaning mega-blunders made by overly zealous sales reps:

A.) When they get the directory for, say, the local HR association, they start contacting people by phone, saying, "<u>Hi, I'm a member of the association, I saw your information in the directory and I thought I'd give you a call.</u>" **This is the quickest way to get kicked out of any type of trade association.**

B.) The other mega-blunder involves an attempt to connect through LinkedIn <u>before we've ever had a conversation with them</u>. This is where a zealous rep makes a LinkedIn connection and immediately sends a message, trying to sell them. That's the last thing we want to do because the other person sees your message and immediately thinks, "Oh great, I just accepted a connection request from another annoying sales person who's now trying to sell me."

If you lack a LinkedIn Premium account or you have limited InMails, the easiest way to reach out to LinkedIn prospects is to become a member of as many **groups** as possible. On LinkedIn you can max out at 50 groups (more if you belong to sub-groups). Look for groups containing your suspects and prospects as members and join. It's easy, and once you do, you can go into that particular group, send that person an email and it won't cost you an In-Mail.

Note: LinkedIn continues to limit this function as well. As of this publishing, you are limited to five messages a month through groups you belong to.

Essential Definitions

Now you've seen clearly defined examples of the three most important types of contacts encountered during the sales process: Suspects, Prospects and Targets.

By now, you can understand why it's so essential to define each one, why you need to fully develop each individual relationship, and how to advance your valuable contact through the hierarchy - in order to ensure the best possible outcome. As you do, you may spot an increasing array of opportunities that make the process even more valuable…as you continue to cultivate a long-term relationship.

Here again, it's important to remember that we're dealing with people… just people. We aren't trying to erect an office building or engineer a rocket launch, which require mechanics and a host of materials. Too often, sales people reduce prospects to object-status as they try to pump up a scattergun approach to selling. They think they can succeed while making only one-touch contacts and pressuring them into appointments, which essentially de-humanizes the interaction. While this might work at times, if you dedicate yourself to this approach you risk losing a lot of potentially lucrative suspects. You may win a battle or two, but ultimately you're going to lose the war.

Differentiating between the three arch-typical stages of interaction - Suspect, Prospect and Target - will hopefully change the way you think: not only about your approach, but how you follow-through and take full advantage of **_every_ opportunity** that comes your way.

In the following chapter, you will see how it all comes together in a streamlined system of relational development as you discover a new sense of daily purpose. Along the way, I will introduce new levels of finesse to the approach of every prospect and target you ultimately choose to qualify. That's when you will see just **how easy it is** to build a sustainable system of selling success.

No More Brain-Drain

You will no longer be forced to rely on that relentless, brain-draining, energy-sapping, rejection-fraught scattergun approach to landing appointments and making deals. Time to move on! I've seen too many talented people slog down the old road of random cold-calling, which is unsustainable over a long period of time. The end-result for many a great sales professional has, unfortunately, been unnecessary burn-out and even premature abandonment of a lucrative, fulfilling career. What these individuals really needed all along was nothing more than an easy way to re-structure and re-think the way he or she was selling!

That's precisely where we're going in the next chapter. Once you make the paradigm shift as outlined in the next few pages, you will begin to envision a new future as you take the most direct path to ongoing, sustained success.

CHAPTER FOUR

The 10-Week, 12-Touch Sales Campaign

Before we begin, please know that this honed, streamlined and thoroughly developed selling process is based on decades of research and practical application in the field, including years and years of my personal sales experience, and the experience of highly gifted people I have managed and coached. It isn't untested theory, it isn't rocket science, and it isn't some extreme new approach to selling. It is a proven, structured approach to sales in the staffing industry. It makes sense, and it works – extremely well.

Much of our sales methodology focuses on a variety of studies about the number of times you need to reach out to a prospect before you close a sale. On that note, you might find this interesting: it wasn't too long ago that studies showed it took an average of 6 touches to close a deal. Over time, the frequency rose to 8. Now, recent studies show that <u>it takes 10 to 12 attempts to make a sale</u>.

Here's the problem: most sales people give up after the second or third call. I know this from my experience as an executive for a large staffing firm, and now president of my own company. Over the years, literally thousands of sales people have reached out to me as a suspect, prospect, and target. And the vast majority fall into the same trap…

Most sales people never call me more than <u>once</u>. When I talk to other executives, I ask them how often sales people call and the answer is pretty much uniform across-the-board:

- "<u>I never hear</u> from sales people more than once or twice."
- "<u>It's rare to hear</u> from a sales rep multiple times."
- "I'm more likely to listen to sales people who call many times - regardless of the message - <u>because they're persistent</u>."

Think about it – this is like running the first 20 or 30 yards of a hundred-yard dash, and wondering why you never win the race! The overwhelming majority of sales people - in our industry or any other - aren't persistent enough to be consistently successful. Even those that know they need to be persistent often lack the patience to see a prospect through to close.

Here's the Solution: You need a structured, multi-step process that requires you to be <u>effectively</u> persistent.

Along with an array of other tactical tools, we created this 10-week, 12-step process to do just that. With this process, you will be able to approach prospects in a variety of different ways, understanding that people respond to different types of communication.

For example, I'm far more likely to return an email than a voice mail. Others are more likely to return voice mails right away. Some pick up the phone more frequently than they answer emails – if you send this individual an email, it's lost immediately; but, call them by phone and they'll pick up. And believe it or not, some people respond best if you send them a letter, in an envelope, sent by <u>snail</u> mail. Yes, it's true. It takes all kinds, as they say.

We have repeatedly tested a careful mix of communications designed specifically for our 10-week process. Going back to the chapter titled "Sales is a Game of Chess," each move was taken to build upon the previous one, and as we see each piece of our process as being a kind of chess move, we go through all 12 moves to achieve the final score: a win. That's how it works. Let's get started.

Value Prop Mailing

Week One

Beginning with Week One, we're going to start off with a letter. This is where a lot of people say "Snail-mail? Really? You want <u>me</u> to send a letter? Aren't we beyond that?" No, we are not at all beyond that. We've come full circle. In fact, this critical piece has suddenly become quite innovative, believe it or not. Why?

- One, it gives us the opportunity to craft and deliver our message tangibly – in a medium that our prospect can actually touch and feel
- Two, U.S. Postal Service volume has declined significantly over the last 10 years, so there is less competition for our prospect's attention than any other communication method
- Three, it is extremely rare to hear of anyone in staffing company sales mailing anything other than maybe an occasional postcard. From my experience, I would say less than 1 or 2% of our industry regularly sends an actual letter.

So, we do something else entirely. What we do is actually mail a letter that talks about our Value Proposition. Remember this one? We talked about it earlier. It's made of our differentiators – those things that truly separate us from competitors and resonate with prospects. We also do it because we face a lot less noise when competing via real-mail versus email. Think about it: the average person gets maybe five or six pieces of actual paper mail a day; a "really busy person" may get 10 to 15 pieces of mail daily.

Yet, the average "really busy person" gets an eye-glazing 200 to 300 emails a day or more, as he or she simultaneously tries to handle 30 to 40 phone calls, a barrage of texts, numerous instant messages, and an array of social media posts and messages…in one, single day.

Snail Power

Postal mail has become a much less crowded form of communication. A piece of mail is something tangible and tactile, and, if done right, it allows us to appear professional rather than transactional. It allows some branding and name recognition, but even more important than that, we can say <u>exactly</u> what we want to say. Whereas in a voice mail let's face it, we run the risk of stumbling all over ourselves, wandering here and there in an ad-lib effort to leave the type of voice mail we want to leave.

A well-crafted letter will say it for us, and it gives us the opportunity to establish our credibility and differentiators <u>before</u> we pick up the phone.

Now at this point, you may be saying "I don't even look at my mail, and many of my clients and prospects have somebody else look at theirs." And you would be right. But remember two things. One, this isn't about you and how you prefer to communicate. It's about approaching our suspects in a variety of ways so we find the one that works the best for

THEM. And two, this is just one step in the process. There is no silver bullet that works for everyone. You will lose suspects in each step of the process, and that's ok. But for some of your suspects, I guarantee that this letter is what will get their attention, and ultimately get you the sale.

Letter Ingredients

1.) Your Week One Value Prop mailing essentially starts off to say, "Hello (Name of Prospect), I'm reaching out to introduce myself and my company. I realize that you get a lot of emails, phone calls and even letters from other staffing firms, so let me take just a moment of your time to show why we're different." (We want to let them know that *we know* how busy they are. We also let them know that we're not living in a vacuum, that we know we're not the only sales rep in the universe.)

2.) Then we demonstrate why we're different with a few strong, bullet-point differentiators – to be covered in more detail, shortly.

3.) Then we wind it up with an open door: "I'll reach out to you next week and see if we can talk briefly by phone - maybe 10 to 15 minutes – so I can find out if we might be a solution for you now or in the future."

4.) Your letter also should contain a second document that establishes proof for your message, which could include:
    - Client testimonials reinforcing your differentiators and Value Prop.
    - A short case-study showing significant, tangible, quantifiable improvements you were able to provide for a client company.
    - A page talking about the tenure of your clients, especially if you have big-name-recognizable clients we call "logo" accounts. ("Logo" accounts are especially persuasive, demonstrating your

credibility because well-respected companies have entrusted you with their staffing needs.)

Subtle Differentiators

The following mailing tips might sound a bit silly but ***they absolutely work***. We want to get as far away as possible from the mass-mail look, and we do it in a couple of different ways.

First, <u>address the envelope by hand</u>. If you think about it, when you get a stack of mail what's the first thing you look for? If you're like me, you look for anything from a human being, anything personalized. Everything else looks like mass mail and goes into the back of the stack, or into the trash, without a second look.

Second, and again this might sound a bit unusual, but it <u>really works</u>. We have seen over and over again that using big, interesting stamps can catch the prospect's attention. Rather than use the standard Forever-type stamp with the familiar flag, or some other generic stamp that comes in a roll of 50, we go down to the post office and ask for the **biggest**, **brightest**, **gaudiest**, **most unique**, **most interesting stamps** available. I know it sounds trivial, but this simple step actually triggers feedback. People respond to outlandish stamps because they are so used to the same old boring mail.

Here's another trick, one I've used many times. During major holidays, **buy lots of holiday stamps**. Then **wait until June to use them**. When you do, people literally call you up laughing, anxious to let you know that you sent a Santa stamp on the Fourth of July.

Here's your response (chuckling): "Well, it worked, right?"

Those are some of the variations on the general theme of Week One Value Prop Mailing.

Week Two

In Week Two, we'll <u>reach out a total of **three** times</u>.

1.) We begin with a **follow-up email** saying something like: "I sent you a letter last week and I know you're busy, so you may not have had a chance to read it. Let me briefly re-cap what it says." (Your follow-up email moves quickly through the bullet points in last week's letter.)

At the end of the follow-up email in Week Two, add, "I'm going to reach out to you tomorrow." Then set a specific time frame for tomorrow's call. It's important to give yourself enough room the next day for interruptions in your own schedule. You might accordingly set a two-hour window - maybe between 2:00 p.m. and 4:00 p.m. – to make sure you'll be able to make that call.

It's critical in this process to always do what you say you are going to do, no matter how small it may be. From the very beginning, it shows that you are the kind of person who will actually follow-up and get things done. If you don't, it could establish all sorts of subconsciously (or not so subconscious) negative impressions in the mind of a prospect, namely that: a.) you might lack punctuality in general, b.) that you might promise without delivery and, c.) that if you can't keep your own scheduled appointment, you may act irresponsibly in other ways.

2.) We **call** the next day (when we said we would) and leave a brief message, something like,

"This is {name} with {company}, and this is a follow-up on an email and letter I sent you a few days ago. In case you haven't had a chance to look at them, both talk about some of the areas that make us different from other firms and how those differences benefit our clients. For example, {briefly describe your top differentiator}.

"I would love to have the opportunity to learn more about your recruitment strategy and see if our unique approach might be a solution for you. I'm going to follow up with an email to see if I can schedule a 15-minute phone call on your calendar, this week or next. I look forward to speaking with you."

3.) Later that day, we send a **follow-up email** that reads: "Hi, I just left you a voice mail and wanted to see if I could get 10-15 minutes on your calendar for a call this week or next. Please let me know a couple good times on your schedule."

In Summary, during your Week Two outreach you should:

- **Send a follow-up email to the letter**
- **Call the next day**
- **Send a follow-up email to the voice mail**

[NOTE: By the way, if, during any part of this process we get any return communication, good or bad, we immediately pull them out of the 10-week process. If we qualified them as a prospect or a target, we move to the sales process. If we disqualify them, we remove them altogether. And if they are still a suspect because we don't have enough information to qualify or disqualify them, we keep them as a suspect and move them back to a quarterly contact.]

Week Three

If we haven't heard from the prospect by Week Three, we leave another **voice mail** saying:

"This is {first name} with {Company}. I just want to follow up on my previous communications to see if I could speak briefly with you about your recruiting strategy and our unique approach to staffing. I can be reached at {phone number}. I'll follow up with an email next week in case that is easier for you."

Week Four

In Week Four, we do another very brief follow-up **email** with a new and compelling variation. We quickly remind them that this week's email is a follow-up email from the week prior, but now we **add a testimonial** from one of our clients. I call it a "compelling variation" because people like to read third-party opinions and reviews. I know I do. This testimonial will reinforce things that make us different from our competitors. "Don't believe me – believe one of my clients."

Week Five

We send a follow-up **voice mail** in Week 5 and mention last week's testimonial, adding that more information/testimonials/differentiators are available upon request.

Week Six

In Week Six, we shift gears and leave an **email about being "in your area."** It could sound like this:

"I'm going to be in your area next {day} and wanted to see if I could stop in to introduce myself.

I know you are busy, but thought it would a great opportunity for us to meet briefly in person.

Let me know when you have 10-15 minutes between {hour range} and I'll make sure to drop by.

[NOTE: We are NOT asking for a meeting. We're simply saying: we will be in their area; we're just asking to stop by and introduce ourselves. This is a tactical and psychological difference, in that we are asking for a lesser perceived commitment than a meeting.]

Week Seven

If you haven't heard from them by now, simply **call and remind** them that you're going to be in their area. We've found that even when people don't answer our requests for the drop-by, we might get messages from suspects or their executive assistant, saying, "I'm sorry we're not going to be available that day. Can we meet another day?"

Now we're getting more than a response - we're actually getting an *apology* because they aren't available. This is means that we have changed the dynamics to an unspoken relationship with our suspect... even before we've started talking to them. At this point, it's as if they've already started to get to know us <u>because we've been consistently reaching out to them</u>.

We're not just hammering them with email after email, like so many sales people tend to do. Our suspects and prospects recognize that repetitive email campaigns go out to hundreds of people, so by mixing up the communication method week after week, we are further differentiating ourselves and creating a familiarity with our suspects and prospects.

- **We're adding a touch of personalized variation to our communications.**
- **We've sent a hand-addressed letter that feels more personal, less like mass-mail.**
- **We're sending emails followed by appropriately-timed phone calls**
- **We're demonstrating that we are not part of some automated mass-marketing system.**
- **At this point, the sum total of our overall messaging says, "Hey, I'm actually a real person!"**

If we've done a good job of messaging, if we've created compelling Value Prop with testimonials and other differentiators, our messaging is bound to be stronger than our competitors. We've successfully differentiated ourselves from other staffing companies. We have given them the feeling that we're taking the time to personally reach out to them, and our message is different.

By the way, if you are selling nationally rather than locally, then the "in your area" approach doesn't make much sense. In that case, week 6 and 7 can easily be replaced with additional content. We have separate sample scripts available for sales people that don't sell locally.

Caution: Avoid "Jump-the-Gun" Meltdown

- If you haven't seen a response at this point, don't stop.
- We're trying to establish in their minds that we are above vendor status.
- We want to show that we're at a higher "consultative" level.
- We've invested a lot of extra time, done a lot of work - far more than most reps.

This is where some sales people get impatient and <u>blow it</u>!

By now, most sales reps (and sales managers) are getting impatient. At this point, they may be thinking: *"This isn't working – I still haven't talked to most of these people. Even if they don't respond to my 'In-Your-Area Voice Mail,' I'm going to go ahead and show up."*

Don't do it! You've spent all this time and effort building your credibility and differentiating yourself, and now you're going to act like the stereotypical sales person. This kind of jump-the-gun-meltdown looks like any number of things to suspects and prospects: desperation, impulsiveness, rudeness, recklessness, or just another typical sales rep in the staffing industry. In other words, it destroys everything the sales person has tried to do, putting them in the same category as all the rest. After all that work, the rep once again becomes "just another" staffing vendor. And I'm hoping that, at this point, you don't want to be seen as just another vendor (although if you did feel that way, you probably would have stopped reading by now).

Week Eight

By Week Eight we reach out with **an email that provides relevant content**. Content marketing refers to any type of material that positions you as a subject matter expert, including white papers, e-books, blogs, and articles. If your company hosts seminars and webinars, let them know and send an invitation for them to participate. A variety of different things can be done from a content standpoint.

Even if your company has no content (which, frankly, most staffing companies rarely provide) you can find relevant articles on Google, LinkedIn, or on an association web site related to your target industry.

Once you locate appropriate content, always note the source and forward the content as an FYI. Along with the content add a quick note, like, "I ran across this article and I thought of you. Here's how it applies to what I've been saying." Again, make sure the content will be relevant to them and what they do. If it's "news they can use," it will reinforce your value because the content has value to them. Ultimately, when you send them valued, relevant content, you become a resource, rather than just-another-sales-person. (and it sure beats "Hi it's me again, just checking in!)

Quick Tip for <u>Finding "Relevant" Content</u>

Go to **Google Alerts** and type in search criteria based on key words relevant to your suspects and prospects. If you're going after manufacturing, search for articles related to, say, manufacturing-employment. If your niche is manufacturing in Chicago, make your search relevant locally as well. Search for content about "Chicago manufacturing employment." Google Alerts will give you a preview of the search results. Once you get the results you're looking for, save the search and sign up for email alerts based on that kind of content, every day. Now you have a steady flow of content delivered to you, with little effort.

Week Nine

As we wind down our 10-week campaign, we leave a **light-hearted "persistent" voice mail**. It should go something like this:

"Well, at this point I feel pretty confident that you can't say I'm not persistent! This is {first name} with {Company}. I feel like I know your voice mail well enough now, so it would be great to get a chance to speak with you as well. Feel free to call me at {phone} or email me at {email} if you'd like to set up a brief call."

Week Ten

'The Take-Away'

Week Ten is different. This is when we send out what we call our **"backing-off email."** This is where we startle them a little and tell them we're going away (at least for now).

"Backing-Off" Email Text:

In this email, we say:

"Over the last 10 weeks, I've come to the realization that you either don't have a need for staffing, are thrilled with your current situation, or I haven't effectively communicated the value that we can provide.

And while I pride myself on being persistent, I certainly don't want to come across as a pest. So, I'm going to back off reaching out for now.

If your situation changes and you would like to talk about your staffing needs and how we might help, I will be thrilled to talk with you. Otherwise, I'll plan on reaching out in a few months to keep in touch and see if it makes more sense for us to talk then."

The Turn-Around

This very often sparks an abrupt turn-around. After sending the Backing-Off message, what we often see is a radical change of heart. Suspects and prospects that have ignored us throughout the process often reach back out (sometimes even apologizing), and suddenly start talking about their situation. In many cases, the backing-off email sparks appointments and even orders.

Not to get too deeply into the psychology angle, but let's go back in time to your high school days when someone had a crush on you, or vice-versa. Maybe the one who had the crush was just an annoyance. But in the back of your mind it was sort of flattering too…until one day you found that they no longer had a crush on you. All of a sudden, they became more interesting.

The same psychological pattern applies to sales when we offer, offer, offer – then we take it away. Suddenly they're thinking, "Now that you're not going to reach out to me anymore, I actually do kind of want to talk to you…so, now I'm going to respond."

This step in the process is based on the well-established psychological concept of 'reactance'. As human beings, we like having options. When our options are reduced, or eliminated by others, we tend to have a strong emotional reaction. Even though we're just a sales person who's been calling on them for the last 10 weeks, we are still taking away one of their options. If they have had any interest in our message up to this point, they will be likely to respond to this message. Not only have we seen this happen over and over again with suspects in the campaign, but I've spoken with many of my clients that admit to responding to this sales tactic as well.

We have seen this happen over, and over…and over again!

****

You'll find these and other secrets addressed in more detail throughout our staffing sales training programs, online blogs, web articles, books and other materials. I wish we had enough space to fit it all in, but we'd run through too many volumes and your eyes would glaze over. You would miss the essentials.

Instead we've carefully selected and condensed the essentials in a form that you can put to immediate use…and prosper. Then we put it all into this little book so you could easily cut-to-the-chase and get started.

The 'Getting-Started' Formula

After you do some hands-on work with this easy-to-use process and get the hang of it, after you get the feel for the cadence of the process, you will see how powerful this system can be. Your results will grow dramatically. Your self-confidence will grow with the momentum the process creates. But it's just as important to give it enough of a jump-start to make it happen.

If you are a full-time, dedicated sales rep, I recommend sending out 50 Value Prop mailings a week (if you're not 100% dedicated to sales in your role, then pro-rate the number accordingly). Each week you will add another 50 suspects to the process. Don't plunge in and try for 300 mailings at once because it's too overwhelming, and it further promotes the sales rollercoaster effect we talked about. Just pace yourself and stagger your contacts.

Now you may be thinking: "*Wait, if I start 50 new suspects each week, at the end of 10 weeks I'll be trying to keep up with 500 contacts!*" Actually, you won't. We have found that over the course of 10 weeks, you will communicate with over 90% of the suspects. And remember, when you do interact with a suspect, positive or negative, you remove them from the process. Plus, you aren't calling every suspect every week. So even when you have 10 campaigns going at the same time, you are only making 200 calls a week, at most (usually less due to the attrition we just discussed). This is a manageable number for a dedicated sales person, and ensures that you are consistently hitting the activity numbers needed to be successful.

We have links to spreadsheets and other tools that will keep you on track and, in no time, this will be such an ingrained, structured approach to your prospecting activity that you will wonder how you ever sold before implementing it.

Ultimate Success Driver

Let this become THE process driving your ultimate success in sales. My process is not meant to simply supplement what you do, it is meant to become the way you do it…for yourself, for your organization, for your future in sales, wherever you go.

You will touch your suspects and prospects 12 times during our 10-week process (which includes three "touches" in week 2). You will pursue your prospects for 10 weeks, and you should do it with confidence - because it really works! After you have this process up and running, keep in mind that we have seen the very same process generate career-changing results. I'm talking about measurable results involving hundreds of sales people in the staffing industry.

But **this is the very first time I have ever presented my proven success formula** in such a concisely honed and practical package… in the pages of an easily read, quickly digestible book you can take anywhere for future reference.

Because it circumvents the traditionally stressful (and unsuccessful) selling process, my process will give you and your organization a substantial competitive advantage in the staffing industry. With a tweak here and there, you will find it portable enough to work well in many industries as well. I've introduced this process to many sales organizations outside the staffing industry, and believe me, everything still applies. This is because the process is all about initiating and establishing contact, reinforcing compelling messaging, maintaining contact, and differentiating yourself from the competition - with consistency and enough variety to keep your voice from sounding repetitive.

If you take the time to implement, and are persistent in its execution, you will have the best in class sales process in the staffing industry. Also rest assured that if you choose not to use it, your competition certainly will. Somebody (you or your competition) is going to adapt and win the staffing sales game, so please get started right away and welcome aboard!

All…or nothing

If you want this program to work, you can't just cherry-pick certain parts and ignore the rest. It only works when you use ALL of it.

Please don't jump off on Week 4 after giving it a couple of tries, and try to jump back in later in the middle of the process. That's like skipping your turn a couple times in chess and still thinking you can win. I have seen over and over that when this process fails, it is for two reasons; it was never implemented completely, and/or it was abandoned too early. This is all about carefully timed momentum and the prospect's perception of personalized messaging. In other words, if you want to give a convincing performance you need to "stick with the script," Only then will you sell your message and get results.

Drowning in the "Cycle"

I know how tough the selling process can be when you're out there on your own, flailing away at doors that never seem to open. I personally have experienced what it's like when we find ourselves slowly drowning in what I call the Push-and-Rejection Cycle, the old "Cycle" that can send even the most motivated sales people to the sidelines. Instead, think of my program as a kind of a drown-proofing system with a constantly refreshing flow of new prospects – a self-refreshing flow that will keep your pool actively filled with suspects. This is what will keep you afloat when others fall into yet another drought.

I hope this book has given you a game-changing new perspective, along with everything you need to repeatedly generate new wins. Now it's time for the final moves on the chess board. Now that we've initiated contact, qualified our suspect into a prospect, and piqued that prospect's interest, how do we effectively manage and lead them through the rest of the sales process to become a new client?

In the next chapter, I will show you how to put it all together…in a durable formula designed to *last a lifetime*!

CHAPTER FIVE

Managing Your Pipeline

We've talked about the 10-week prospecting campaign, which really is a structured prospecting system. It creates a solid structure so you can easily qualify and disqualify suspects. It will turn a good many qualified suspects into prospects, and we will disqualify many of them as well.

The best remaining few are going to float to the top of the pool and become actual **targets**.

In a way, this is really where the true sales process begins. This is because targets generate the opportunities in our pipeline, and that's what we're going to focus on in this chapter. But first, what is a pipeline? What are opportunities? And why is 'pipeline management' such a critical sales tool?

Inside the Pipeline

The so-called 'pipeline' is really just a list of sales opportunities. A productive sales professional works closely on his or her pipeline because every item in the pipeline represents an opportunity which, in turn, lives in a defined stage of the sales process. By the way, you may hear different terms for essentially the same thing, with it often being referred to as a "funnel," for example, but sales funnels and sales pipelines are just different terms for the same thing.

Why use a pipeline? First, we manage opportunities more effectively because the pipeline gives us the ability to see everything we need to work on, all at once, and in perspective. It allows us to think more methodically, and strategically, about every available opportunity, rather than grasping at straws in an ad hoc, piece-meal manner.

When an opportunity first becomes part of our pipeline, there are certain things we need to think about. For example, we need to look at the total scope and size of the opportunity (not just an order) as we fully define its true potential. This gives us a better sense of the true value of the opportunity, and how we should prioritize it in relation to other opportunities, while giving us an indication of <u>what we need to do next</u>.

We think of all these things before we ever put an opportunity in our pipeline and by doing just that, we not only define the opportunity, we improve our forward thinking and future planning. In short, everything we do becomes more streamlined, while time becomes more efficiently managed, all because our opportunities are viewed in the appropriate perspective when they are in the pipeline.

Pipeline in Motion

Here's a working example of a Pipeline in Motion: Let's say we're going through our sales process. We've been reaching out to this contact at that suspect company. Finally, they answer the phone and say, "We've been getting your information, we think it's interesting, and we might need ten people for a project a couple of months from now."

In the traditional, shotgun sales cycle – meaning the old, non-managed sales process – a sales person typically says, "Okay, great, I'll try to get an appointment." They may or may not add a follow-up reminder in their planner because they don't give much thought to the opportunity. Instead (as usual) they focus on getting just this one meeting. So, let's say they have their meeting and the contact says, "Okay, thanks, why don't you reach out to me in a couple of weeks? Then we'll see where we are." Well, in the traditional sales playbook, this sometimes means a loss. The sales person may not even put a follow-up in his calendar or task list, thus running the risk of letting the opportunity fade. **This is how we lose momentum**, eventually losing track of the opportunity altogether until it slips through the cracks.

With a pipeline, you have that same scenario, you talk to that person on the phone, you schedule the appointment. But now, you go into your pipeline and create a new opportunity, and you do this typically through your Applicant Tracking System (ATS) or a Customer Relationship Management (CRM) system.

As staffing people know well, an ATS is the primary software used by staffing companies for tracking candidates, orders, companies and contacts. It is the primary software utilized for managing all recruiting and client management efforts, sometimes even payroll and billing. Some have varying degrees of CRM capabilities, some have none at all, leading many firms to resort to separate ways of managing their sales activity - such as Salesforce.com, spreadsheets, Outlook, etc. In most cases the process is, at best, unstructured, increasing the likelihood that potentially lucrative opportunities will be lost in the shuffle.

Back to our suspect company in a managed pipeline: because they think they may need 10 people in two months, we schedule a meeting, get off the call, go into our pipeline and log an opportunity into the system.

Visibility

As we think about that, we look at where we are in the selling process. At the moment, we have very little information about the situation above. But because it's in our pipeline, we then look at the next steps needed to move it through the process. It now has visibility for me and my manager. Now we can review it in the pipeline on a regular basis and make sure we are taking the appropriate next steps.

To really utilize the pipeline to its fullest potential, you need to maximize its visibility and watch it on a daily basis. People who do this have it up on their computers, all day, as they track companies in the sales process. It becomes part of their everyday routine, much the same as their email program. Now they have a better way to monitor the value of an opportunity and manage their time more efficiently. If they have a pending opportunity to staff 10 people in one company – versus one person in another company – they know to allocate more time for the larger opportunity. So, pipeline management allows us to:

- **Monitor where we are in the sales process**
- **Know the next steps we need to take**
- **Prioritize our selling time**
- **Prevent deals from falling through the cracks**
- **Prevent deals from losing momentum – the biggest killer of all.**

Sales people lose way more deals to momentum loss than they do to competition. When I talk to sales people, they say most deals are lost because they lose steam and just fade away. The once-excited prospect loses the sense of importance for the deal because we failed to stay on top of it. <u>We</u> lost momentum, which ultimately lost the deal.

Pipelines Keep Things 'Front of Mind'

Pipelines show us the Big Picture. They keep us from thinking small-time-transactional. If, for example, a contact tells a sales rep about two staff positions, the rep becomes locked onto only those two positions… <u>without</u> keeping a watchful eye on the total opportunity. Meanwhile, the same company may use dozens, or hundreds, of contract employees. But obsessing on just two staff positions, this transactional rep never enters into conversations about the bigger opportunity.

If the rep instead sees the Big Picture and uses the two initial orders primarily to show value, he is ready to move into consultative discussions focused on total, potential opportunities from that contact, department or the entire company. This is how two positions turn into multi-million dollar clients. Properly utilizing a pipeline will encourage sales people to look at the entirety of opportunities, not just the initial job order.

G.E. versus Joe's Body Shop

Let me give you an example. Let's say you're in discussions with a contact at General Electric who wants one accountant. At the same time, you're talking to Joe's Body Shop, which also wants one accountant. If you think transactionally, they look like the same opportunity. Now, change your perspective and look at the Big Picture. Which one has the bigger opportunity? General Electric, of course, which could become a quota-busting, perhaps career-making client for you. Whereas Joe's Body Shop needs one accountant to do the paperwork for 90 days before they hire them, and that's it.

The pipeline treats those two opportunities very, very differently. It causes you to treat them differently while demanding a much different approach. It requires placing more value on the GE opportunity versus the one-time deal at Joe's Body Shop. <u>That's the importance of a pipeline</u>.

Glancing back at Chapter Three and the Suspect/Prospect/Target process, remember that <u>Suspects</u> are companies/contacts that are still unqualified prospects; we probably haven't had a single conversation with them. <u>Prospects</u> are qualified companies/contacts because we know they utilize or need staffing services, but we don't have a current opportunity to work with them; maybe we've had conversations with them but we lack traction, the door hasn't opened.

Conversely, we've had conversations with <u>Targets</u> who have demonstrated an opportunity for us to do business with them, and in the foreseeable future. Even if it's only a slight opportunity, generated by a phone conversation indicating that they "might" need a few people in a couple of months, it's an opportunity. They're open to having more conversations with us, and they are worth us investing more time with them. Those are targets.

Merging Targets with Pipelines

To become a qualified target, the contact or company must have one or more corresponding opportunities in your pipeline. The ideal pipeline should take on the shape of a funnel – bigger at the top, and progressively smaller on down to the bottom (this is, not surprisingly, why pipelines are often called funnels). This happens because we start with more qualified opportunities at the top and, as we go through the sales process, opportunities fall out to leave fewer opportunities at the bottom.

To illustrate, here's how the contact status of Target correlates to the pipeline.

Pipeline Management...a Universal Tool

Pipeline management is nothing new, and I certainly am not taking credit for it. Millions of sales professionals utilize this method every day to more effectively manage their sales process. However, based on over 20 years of sales and sales management experience in the staffing industry, I have found that the following stages are the most relevant to selling in our industry. And while pipeline management is a powerful sales tool for any level of staffing sales, it becomes increasingly important as you rise into complex, high-volume, national account sales, large account sales and "statement of work" projects...because they will require more stages, more contacts, more detailed analysis.

We'll go through each stage and its meaning shortly, but just to recap here's the point: a prospect becomes a target only when it has a corresponding opportunity in the pipeline. These must fall into one of the following stages.

The first stage is "Qualified," then "Solution Developed" and "Proposal Presented," followed by "Negotiate and Close" and "Fulfillment," until we reach the final "Won or Lost" moment in the end-game. Now let's examine individual aspects of each stage.

Stage 1: Qualified

To enter the "qualified" stage, the first stage in the pipeline, we need some reason to believe that we have a chance to do business with a contact. To quote the immortal Lloyd Christmas in the movie *Dumb and Dumber*, "So you're saying there's a chance!" This almost always occurs when we've had a conversation with a contact in the organization, they have indicated that they have a potential need, and are open to the idea of talking with us. Oftentimes details are fairly vague at this point because we have relatively little information about the opportunity. But the door has cracked open. To be considered a qualified opportunity, we must have had at least one phone, email, or in person conversation with a contact. Whatever the case, this kind of activity warrants follow-up.

At this point, we probably only have a 10% to 20% chance of actually winning the business and generating revenue. We know relatively little about the opportunity, but we want to get it into the pipeline so we can have that all-important visibility. This is the 'Qualified' stage and this is where we begin to move it through the pipeline.

Stage 2: Solution Developed

At this stage, we've met with the prospect and have done a needs analysis. We now understand what they need, and for that need we believe we have a solution. So, if we use the same scenario – they need 10 people in a couple of months – we meet with them and go through an interview to ask qualifying questions. This is when we get more info about their needs, more about their pain points, and some idea of their past experiences. Questions asked at this stage might include:

- "What type of skill sets do you use staffing for?"

- "What challenges have you experienced/are you experiencing with your staffing model?"
- "Is that the model you want to use?"
- "What is compelling you to consider alternative solutions?"
- "How are these issues impacting your business?"

Once we have answers, we then make a final determination of the solution we can provide for them. We're in the "Solution Developed" stage, which means that...

- **We have a strong understanding of their staffing needs**
- **We have a clearer picture of their current situation**
- **We are confident that we have a solution to meet those needs and goals**

The minimum activity in this stage would include one or more in-person meetings. If you're a sales person selling nationally, or selling outside your market – maybe a Denver sales rep going after an Atlanta company - it may not be possible to have an in-person meeting, but it would be some kind of formal meeting, like a scheduled phone or web conference. If, however, you're in a more accessible local or regional situation, you would probably have an in-person meeting. Either way, in this stage we typically would put our odds at a 30% to 40% chance of winning the business. Now it's time to present a proposal.

Stage 3: Proposal Presented

The "Proposal Presented" stage means just what it says - that our proposal has been presented in one form or another. It could be presented in a variety of different ways including a formal proposal, a presentation, a staffing agreement or contract, a statement of work, or even just an email with a price quote.

Regardless of the delivery method, we've submitted rates and proposed our solution. Minimum activity here would include one or two in-person meetings, maybe more. With very small deals, we might even present our proposal without an actual in-person meeting. If they need a receptionist next week, for example, and ask for pricing, a simple email or verbal quote may be enough. But in most cases, you have had one or two meetings with them, and at this point you're closing in on the deal. Your chances of success are typically in the 50% to 60% range. Now, your next step is to negotiate and close.

Stage 4: Negotiate and Close

We're here at last. They want to work with us. They like the price (for the most part). They agree with what we're saying. We've presented a proposal and a formal agreement.

The deal could still be under formal review. Maybe they want to tweak a few things and negotiations are moving forward, or we still don't know if they'll be coming back to us for more negotiations – which can be the case when it's going through legal, HR, or purchasing. At this stage, we typically have a 70-80% probability of winning the deal.

Stage 5: Fulfillment

This stage is pretty unique to staffing. In most industries, you would move from Negotiate & Close to Win. A signed contract means you landed the deal and now you just have to deliver the goods or services.

However, in staffing we know it's not that simple. A lot can happen, and go wrong, between the signed contract and actually generating revenue. Lack of qualified candidates, no shows, positions filled by other firms or the client, and changes to client priorities have all derailed deals after the contract comes back. I could wallpaper my house with all the signed contracts I've received over the years that never generated revenue (although I don't think my wife would approve of the look).

So we've added another stage to the pipeline – Fulfillment. This stage occurs after the client has signed and returned the contract, and before our first employee starts. We're almost there – we just need to fill the initial position and have someone start billing. Typically we are at a 90-95% probability at this point, although that could vary based on the difficulty of the position and other factors, including those mentioned above.

Won or Lost: 100% - 0% Probability

Wherever we may be in the process, we're ready to close it out of the pipeline as being either Won or Lost. **A win means that we are now generating revenue, and of course we all know what lost means (as difficult as that is for most of us sales people to admit).** The final stage of the pipeline hierarchy needs to be noted accordingly.

CHAPTER SIX

Fine-tune Your Pipeline

Establishing Deal Value

How do we establish deal value? This is one area of pipeline management that makes sales people nervous because, in our industry, it can very difficult to accurately forecast what an opportunity is worth. Unlike, say, copier sales people - who know the value of a copier to the penny and can get a pretty good sense of how many copiers that company would need – it can be hard for us to establish a comparatively reliable deal value.

With staffing, our prospects often have no idea how much staff they are going to need. Andy how we initially perform can have a profound impact on the actual realized revenue from a deal. While we might have a $500,000 opportunity in the beginning, if we fail to fill that first job, we might lose the opportunity to fill all the other positions. Conversely, we might have what we initially see as a $100,000 opportunity, but because we do such a great job of finding talent, they start feeding us more and more business. That's reality in our industry, and it makes it trickier to accurately estimate deal value.

Add a host of other variables and no wonder people hesitate to estimate deal value, which can be further adjusted as we go through the process, as value becomes more clarified. Remember G.E versus the auto body shop? The auto body shop value was fairly cut and dried. But GE spends $10's of millions annually on staffing – I mean, where do we begin to calculate untold opportunities?

We need to understand, and be okay with the fact, that we are never going to be 100% accurate in assessing deal value. We also should be comfortable that we will likely need to revise the value as we progress through the pipeline stages and learn more about the prospect's operations and needs. We should be able to make a much better valuation in Negotiate & Close than we did in the Qualified Stage. And that's OK! The key is to be conservative without sandbagging, and to get better over time at forecasting deal values.

Annualized Valuation

I recommend basing the value of the deal on annualized revenue, because typically that aligns with annual sales goals, quotas, and commission plans. Therefore, we want to consider some of the following:

- **How much revenue do we expect to realize in the first 12 months of doing business with them?**
- **At what level does our contact have buying influence?**
- **Department level**
- **Division level with authority over multiple departments?**
- **Or at the corporate level, meaning a CEO, president or owner?**

Maybe we're dealing with human resources or procurement people who may have oversight over everything spent on staffing.

Where to Focus

Think about <u>how your target utilizes staffing</u>, and how you believe you will be integrated into their staffing structure;

- Will we be <u>added</u> to the list?
- Will we <u>replace</u> a vendor on the list?
- Do we have an opportunity to move in, <u>take over</u>, and replace everyone on the list?
  (Obviously, the ideal scenario)

Let's say your target spends $1 million annually in staffing, and they already have four providers. If we replace one provider, it's a $250,000 deal – we get one-fourth of the pie. If they add us as a provider, now it's a $200,000 deal because it's split five ways.

If you go for the whole enchilada, asking to be their sole provider, you might be able to point out that the only reason they've used four providers is that none of them could do the whole job (although you better be ready with plenty of evidence proving you can). If you pull it off, however, this enchilada turns into a $1 million deal. As you can see, understanding the prospect's staffing structure, their intentions, and our opportunity - all play substantially into deal value.

We need to look not only at the number of staffing providers, but how things could develop after we start doing business with them. You can get a better look at the future by asking the right pre-qualifying questions. But as I said before, initial estimated value could change dramatically as we move through, so don't get paralyzed by deal-value early on. Go with your best estimates based on pre-qualifying questions, past experience with similar types of positions, and previous discussions. Then be conservative (but no sandbagging!).

Forecasting

Effective forecasting of your pipeline increases your chances that you exceed your goals. For example, if the average win rate in your pipeline is 20%, and you need to bring in $1 million a year, then you will need $5 million in your pipeline at all times (20% of $5 million = $1million). We also need to think about whether opportunities are projects or contracts of less than a year, and forecast their value appropriately. For example, an accountant at a $50 bill rate would annualize to about $100k, but if they are only working four months during tax season, then we adjust the value accordingly.

License-to-Hunt: Beware

This one can be a voracious time-eater offering little in return, but individual situations might change probabilities of success. If so, it might be well-worth the effort.

'License-to-Hunt' situations involve companies that go out to bid from a vendor list, so let's say one of these companies wants to add to their list of vendors. Well, it might sound great at first, but keep one thing in mind: in many cases, you would have to sell twice.

First, you need to go through the sales process to get on the vendor list...without guaranteed revenues, without orders. If you 'win', you get a 'License to Hunt', meaning you now have the right to go out and start selling all over again to their end users. At this point, you're really just getting started from a sales standpoint.

In other words, after all the effort it took just to get on the list, you now have to go out and sell again to all of the hiring managers. That's why this kind of process can cost you a lot of extra time and effort, and forecasting value can be tricky.

I'll give you a 'real-life' example. I was with a large, national staffing company that was constantly trying to land the large, local university as a client. Each year, the school went out to bid to determine who would be among 20 to 25 staffing companies on their vendor list. We would submit a proposal. Sometimes we would get on the list. Sometimes we wouldn't. When we did, we would get a letter saying, "Congratulations, you are now allowed to go out and talk to our hiring managers and see if they'll work with you." …Great. After all the time it took to finally get on the list, now it was time to go out and pitch, literally, HUNDREDS of hiring managers and department heads. In other words, after the exhausting initial effort, you had to go out and sell again…this time going against 20 to 25 other staffing companies!

To this day, some companies dedicate sales resources just for the university. If, or when, they get on the list, they get to go out and sell, knowing that a huge amount of initial effort could result in zero revenue. Think of it as unlocking a door that leads to hundreds of other locked doors. You need the key to the first door in order to get access to the other ones, but now you are starting over again. As far as recording these opportunities in your pipeline, we recommend listing a license-to-hunt deal as an opportunity with zero revenue. If you "win" that opportunity and make the vendor list, you will create individual opportunities with value as you sell to the hiring managers. This will provide a more realistic forecast of potential revenue in your pipeline.

Now, let's talk about the most common pipeline pitfalls.

Pipeline Pitfalls

Here, I want to point out a few pipeline foibles reps tend to fall into. If any of these sound familiar, don't worry, you're not alone. I'll show you how to fix them:

- Entering Opportunities Too Early or Too Late
- Associating Stages with Probabilities
- Losing Momentum…Momentum Lost
- Holding on Too Long.

"Too Early/Too Late"

The first, and most common, pitfall is to enter opportunities in your pipeline too early or too late. In many cases, I see sales reps enter leads into their pipelines. This is way too early! Maybe a contract employee comes in and says a company he used to work at needs to hire 100 people, adding that they're looking for new staffing providers. Now, we haven't actually talked to anyone in the company, so we don't know if we have an opportunity. But this is when many overeager sales people will put it in their pipeline as an opportunity when it is not.

Again, it won't be an opportunity until we actually talk to somebody in the company who: a.) **confirms** the need to hire people, and, b.) agrees to entertain the idea of working with us.

On the flip-side, some people enter opportunities into their pipeline too late because they don't like the idea that they'll lose 80% of the deals they put in it. Instead, they want to feel like they have a better than 50-50 chance before adding them to the pipeline, which can be a tough habit to break. If we wait until every deal poses better than a 50-50 shot, we miss out on properly managing opportunities through the early stages.

We put opportunities in the pipeline at an earlier stage for a very good reason: **visibility**. Enhanced visibility is the primary advantage of having a pipeline. Visibility gives us a better chance of landing those deals, so you want enter those opportunities as soon as they become qualified opportunities. You need **early pipeline visibility** to really maximize your opportunities. I'll say it again: you need to get those opportunities into your pipeline, a.s.a.p.

Pipeline visibility creates better <u>opportunity</u>, better <u>forecasting</u>, and, most importantly, it <u>allows us to prioritize</u> our deals.

"Associating Stages with Probabilities"

Let's take a closer look at pipeline stages and typical probabilities of success.

To summarize, typical opportunity probabilities are as follows:

Qualified –10 to 20%

Solution Development – 30% to 40%

Proposal Presented – 50% to 60%

Negotiate and Close - 70% to 80%

Fulfillment – a 90-95% probability of winning the deal

These are just guidelines, of course, and a variety of factors influence probabilities. Let's say an opportunity comes from a former client with whom we have a great relationship, who is now the primary contact at a new company. He has 10 positions to fill and wants us to do the job. In this case, we don't know a whole lot about the opportunity, but we are confident we have a pretty good chance of getting the business. The probability of success would certainly be a lot higher than your typical "qualified" 20%.

In another scenario, you've run a company through the whole process, you have an agreement in their hands and you are negotiating to close, but somewhere in the back of your mind you can't understand why they want to leave their incumbent. Meanwhile, your contact remains mum when asked to explain. It seems as if they're going through the motions.

Well, maybe they're doing just that – going out to bid to knock down their incumbent's price. Or, maybe they go out to bid every few years for appearances, which could be the case if procurement is running the bid. So, in this situation, I may be in the Negotiate and Close stage, but it feels more like a 20% to 30% chance of closing the deal.

In other words, don't be rigid with your probabilities attached to stages. Each situation must be individually assessed.

"Momentum Loss"

Momentum Loss happens time and again without pipelines, because we lack visibility. If you count on doing things with certain prospects on a regular basis but have no pipeline, you still run a greater risk of Momentum Loss. Regardless of the nature of your relationship with a prospect, it is critical to maintain weekly communications with any contact that has an opportunity in your pipeline. Your prospect may want a follow-up after his vacation next week, which may be followed by a short week after that, due to a holiday. He says, "Why not reach out to me in three weeks?"

Three weeks is a long time. It's easy to lose momentum in three weeks. So, while we agree to reach out to their timeline, we **find creative ways to stay front-of-mind** with them during the entire three-week period. This could be as simple as emailing over a relevant article. Next, we could invite them to join one of our webinars or seminars. In other words, stay <u>front of mind</u> with them, even when they've asked us to stay away for three weeks. The skill is to avoid the appearance of making unwanted follow-ups. Keep it subtle and non-salesy. Keep it going to avoid losing momentum.

"Holding on Too Long"

I once had a prospect company that did about $1.5 million a year in revenue as a third-party distribution center. I had been working with their owner on the opportunity and we would get close to a deal – even to the point of doing a full credit application. But things kept falling flat for different reasons. Finally, after close to a year, my boss told me that I was no longer allowed to say the words "Click Track." When he said it, I replied, "That's fine, as long as you no longer say the word 'Floodgate'." (Names changed to protect the innocent.)

Here's the point: My manager was doing the same exact thing – holding on too long to a stale opportunity. This is when opportunities run through their typical life cycles as seen below:

Very large potential deals ($3 million-plus revenue) – 6 months to over a year

Larger deals ($500,000 to $3 million) – 6 months

Medium deals (under $500,000) – 90 days

Smaller deals (under $250,000) – 30-60 days

Of course there are variables – not every large deal takes six months, and not every small deal closes in less than 60 days. And deal sizes vary widely by industry vertical. It takes a lot more warehouse employees to reach $1 million than travel doctors. But regardless of size, EVERY opportunity eventually runs through a sales cycle, and often it is due to lost momentum. When the cycle runs its course, you will rarely win the deal. You just don't want to admit it because good sales people hate to admit defeat. But the smart sales person also knows when to cut bait and move on to the next opportunity.

Pipelines and Structured Closings

The pipeline is like a blueprint. It shows you exactly what you need to do, where you should focus your effort, and where you stand with your opportunities. The pipeline structures your approach to show you **how to prioritize your efforts** based on deal size, closing potential and other factors. It is a highly effective tool for maximizing your sales efforts.

Another huge benefit is that we're able to analyze the health of our sales pipeline according to the shape of its funnel, because the acquired shape is based on different stages of your pipeline – from Qualified to Fulfillment. This reflects the health of each stage.

If you wind up with an hourglass-shaped pipeline, for example, you have too little in the middle with too much at the top and bottom. If you have a pear-shaped pipeline, you have too much in the middle and the bottom and too little at the top. Either way, you know you're heading for problems in the future due to an inconsistent flow in the Structured Sales Process. Your pipeline helps identify those problem areas while your Structured Sales Process keeps the engine running smoothly, if properly maintained.

A pipeline **determines optimum time allocation**. If you have a pear-shaped pipeline with most of your deals in negotiate & close and fulfillment, that may sound great because you're going to land a lot of deals. But behind that you have nothing. You will have to start the suspect/prospect process from scratch, all over again, which creates a roller-coaster effect – which, in turn, leaves a lot of sales people missing their sales goals and suffering through commission droughts.

All too often, a rep will get into a surge of momentum, do a bunch of prospecting and throw a bunch of opportunities into their pipeline. Then they work the prospects through the process without re-building new prospects, eventually leaving an empty pipeline. I'm sure many of you know from experience what happens.

Well, it happened to me years and years ago until I solved the problem, and that's why I was determined to develop the very process you're reading about right now.

The pipeline **allows you to manage your flow of sales activities** for a consistent, more dependable flow of income, **which changes everything**. Random, shotgun-transaction selling eventually leads to hand-to-mouth living for a lot of sales people. With consistent income you can save for retirement, build your business, plan for the future. That's why a well-managed pipeline is so critical. It's like recirculating water in a natural lake. You have to keep refreshing the lake to prevent stagnation.

The BIG Six

Remember, all you need to do is utilize a simple Six-Step process incorporating the 10-Week prospecting campaign, and basic pipeline management. As presented earlier in this book, the 'BIG' Six fundamentals include:

1.) **Identify Suspect Companies and Contacts**
2.) **Implement the 10-Week Prospecting Campaign**
3.) **Qualify Prospects and Targets**
4.) **Add Opportunities to the Pipeline**
5.) **Work Opportunities through pipeline stages**
6.) **Close-out Wins and Losses**

(All along the way adding new suspects to replenish the pool.)

CHAPTER SEVEN

Structure a Sales Breakthrough in the Staffing Industry

First, I want to thank you for investing your valuable time to read my book, and thank you in advance for giving my game-changing process a chance to succeed. I truly believe this process has the power to change your life, because we have seen what it has done for so many other sales professionals.

I also want to assure you of one thing: as simple as my Six-Step, 10-Week process may sound, amazing, incredibly, at this writing YOU will be among the few to put it to work – a leader of the pack. Although more and more people will eventually get the word, you will have it down by then. You will have mastered your chess moves. The process will be a no-brainer, a self-perpetuating, income-machine-on-steroids that, in time, will seem to run itself as your business grows.

In other words, you will be so far ahead of the pack, it won't matter who finally gets the word. You will be too far out in front to catch. Trust me. I know this because I have a little secret.

The vast majority of sales people in our industry don't have a defined repeatable process, and most have never utilized a pipeline to manage their sales opportunities. And I'm talking sales people at staffing companies of all different sizes and verticals, from start-ups healthcare staffing firms to national and international companies. Just by implementing and executing our process in this book, you will have a best in class sales methodology that puts you in truly elite company.

By now the old transactional routine must sound primitive. Frankly, it is, if not altogether naïve. Oh, but there they all are...*still* out there flailing away, putting on the pressure, hammering suspects with that sweaty, all-or-nothing, make-or-break, one-time phone pitch - pressure cooked to snag an appointment. Some have bailed on that, instead hoping to eke out a few hits from those relentlessly repetitive, mass e-mailings (and their equally expensive mailing lists).

You have to feel a little sorry for some of them. We all know what happens along the way. We've been there. The rep gets frustrated; the suspect gets downright annoyed; the rep is rejected, insulted or yelled at. Motivation dies. Good people flame out...another day in shotgun sales.

Sometimes we blame it on what we're selling or who we're selling for. So, we move to another company, another sales method, another set of management quotas. But all we're really doing is perpetuating a process within a process destined to fade out entirely in the coming years. We're still in the same old transactional head-banger routine.

Your Ship Awaits, Welcome Aboard

If you're new to sales altogether, if you just came over from selling real estate/insurance/IT, if you happen to be a 35-year veteran of staffing sales and feel like you could refresh your pool of prospects…welcome aboard, your ship awaits. Everything you need is in this book. Just get out there and get started. I suspect this might be the least expensive ticket-to-cruise you have ever purchased.

You won't need new equipment. You won't have to buy fancy new software. You won't need new staff. All you need is yourself and the willingness to change your approach. You will also need the persistence and trust to use the ENTIRE process and let it work. That's the key. Otherwise, nothing can stop you, regardless of what you sell, where you sell, or whomever you plan to sell it to…

We're Here for You

If you get stuck, or find yourself momentarily bogged down somewhere in the process, please don't hesitate to get in touch with us through the following contact information.

Tallann Resources
info@tallannresources.com
614-372-5888

We have also created a web page where you can access all the accompanying documents and tools we reference in this book. Here is the link:

http://go.tallannresources.com/winning-the-staffing-sales-game

I am confident that you, and you alone, can put your own process in motion…starting now! I've seen it work, time and again, for hundreds of individuals and organizations nationwide.

Now you have a whole new set of rules for playing the selling game...
so put away the playing cards and get out the chess set. It's your move.

All My Very Best,
Tom Erb
Founder and President
Tallann Resources